TOTAL
FORGIVENESS
Experience

R.T. KENDALL

with Joel Kilpatrick

Charisma
HOUSE
A STRANG COMPANY

Most STRANG COMMUNICATIONS BOOK GROUP products are available at special quantity discounts for bulk purchase for sales promotions, premiums, fund-raising, and educational needs. For details, write Strang Communications Book Group, 600 Rinehart Road, Lake Mary, Florida 32746, or telephone (407) 333-0600.

TOTAL FORGIVENESS EXPERIENCE by R. T. Kendall
Published by Charisma House
A Strang Company
600 Rinehart Road
Lake Mary, Florida 32746
www.strangbookgroup.com

Unless otherwise noted, all Scripture quotations are from the Holy Bible, New International Version. Copyright © 1973, 1978, 1984, International Bible Society. Used by permission.

Scripture quotations marked KJV are from the King James Version of the Bible.

Library of Congress Catalog Card Number: 2004103419
International Standard Book Number: 978-1-59185-552-1

This publication is translated in Spanish under the title *Perdón total*, copyright ©2004 by R. T. Kendall, published by Casa Creación, a Strang company. All rights reserved.

10 11 12 13 — 13 12 11 10 9
Printed in the United States of America

CONTENTS

INTRODUCTION

THIS BOOK, OUT of all the books I have written, is by far the one that has the greatest potential to heal the human heart. Forgiveness is one of the most needed, relevant subjects Christians can study today, though it is often neglected or put aside. Perhaps it is too difficult, or maybe it has simply fallen out of fashion as a subject of sermons and study guides. But if we remain less-than-expert forgivers, we cripple ourselves in every area of life. Forgiveness should be the very breath of our Christian lives. It is the single key that sets us free to live abundantly, as Jesus promised those who follow Him.

A woman I know named Margaret Moss, whose husband, Norman, was the minister of the Queen's Road Baptist Church in Wimbledon, has given me permission to share the following two forgiveness-related stories. The first concerned a woman who had been in a car accident twenty-two years before. Her neck had been in constant pain for years, and because she could not turn her head to look into the rearview mirror of her car, she had been forced to forfeit her driver's license. Margaret asked if she had ever prayed for the driver of the car who had caused the accident.

"No," was her reply.

Margaret suggested that the woman pray for him.

"I forgive him," the lady began to pray.

"Now bless him," Margaret continued.

The woman began to bless this man, and the pain left. The next morning she could move her neck for the first time in twenty-two years. That was more than a year ago, and the healing has continued.

The second account involved a lady in her forties whose father had terribly abused her. This lady claimed that she had said to the Lord, "I forgive him," again and again. But despite her prayer, she had continued in "heaviness of spirit." Margaret suggested she bless her father as well. The moment the woman said, "I bless my father," the heaviness completely left! The last time Margaret saw this lady, the spirit of heaviness was still gone. The lady told her, "Now my life has completely changed."

Her life changed because she embraced the awesome power of *total forgiveness*. Forgiveness is not total forgiveness until we bless our enemies—and pray for them to be blessed. Forgiving them is a major step; totally forgiving them is fully achieved when we set God free to bless them. But in this, we are the first to be blessed, and those who totally forgive are blessed the most.

This study guide will take you on a journey of total forgiveness, identifying the benefits and stages of forgiveness, the alternatives to forgiveness (there are no good ones!), and practical ways you can liberate your heart from unforgiveness from the past. It will give you opportunity to pause and examine your heart, and then to take action on what you have learned. It will embolden you to live in a new experience of grace and empowerment that may have been absent from your life up to now.

Forgiveness works in all areas of life—from your physical health, to your emotions, to your deepest spiritual life, to your relationships and careers. I have seen the amazing benefits of forgiveness on many different occasions. And, sadly, I have seen the damage done when people don't totally forgive. I pray that no matter what has happened to you, you will see the necessity of forgiving people totally, repeatedly, completely. I pray that this book will exceed all expectations for every person who reads it. It is designed to set people free, so that we may let the past be past…at last.

RT, you must totally forgive them. Until you totally forgive them you will be in chains. Release them, and you will be released.

—JOSIF TSON

CHAPTER 1

CAN YOU LEARN
TO FORGIVE?

THE JUNE 5, 2000 issue of the *London Daily Express* carried an article with this headline: "Can You Learn to Forgive?" It began with the following declaration: "Bearing a grudge can hold you back and even damage your health."[1] The writer of the article, Susan Pape, had interviewed Dr. Ken Hart, a lecturer at Leeds University who had been running the "world's first forgiveness course"—a seminar designed to help people forgive their enemies and let go of their grudges. Participants ranged from a jilted husband to victims of burglary and bullying. They all had one thing in common: they were angry, bitter, and wanted revenge.

PERSONAL REFLECTIONS

1. Have you known people who are tied up in their own knots of bitterness and plots for revenge? How did they get to be that way? Describe a real person you know who fits this description.

   _____

   _____

_____

_____

_____

2. Do you recognize these traits in your own life? Would other people describe you as being angry and bitter? Would they be right? Explain.

_____

_____

_____

_____

_____

WOUNDED CHRISTIANS

Most of us have experienced times in our lives when we are pushed beyond our limits to forgive. Unfortunately, some Christians may lag behind in the area of forgiveness.

I myself was one who was unable to forgive for much of my life. One time I was hurt so deeply that it affected just about every area of my life: my family, my ministry, and my very sense of self-worth. At times I felt like Job when he cried, "I have no peace, no quietness; I have no rest, but only turmoil" (Job 3:26), or like David when he prayed, "Answer me quickly, O LORD; my spirit fails. Do not hide your face from me or I will be like those who go down to the pit" (Ps. 143:7). I doubt that those who brought this situation upon me had any idea what I went through, and I pray they never will.

PERSONAL REFLECTIONS

1. What is the deepest hurt you have experienced? Does it still occupy a place in your life? Is there a "room" in your soul where this wound festers and remains alive? Explain.

_____

_____

_____

_____

_____

My friend Josif Tson, of Romania, spoke some of the most important words anybody has personally shared with me: "RT, you must totally forgive them. Until you totally forgive them you will be in chains. Release them, and you will be released." No one had ever talked to me like that in my life. At first I was angry; I felt hemmed in. But it was a pivotal moment for me, and it changed my life. I realized the Bible is true when it says, "Faithful are the wounds of a friend" (Prov. 27:6, KJV).

I, of all people, should not have needed such a word. Nobody should have had to tell a mature minister of the gospel of Christ the most obvious and fundamental teaching of the New Testament.

Perhaps you feel the same way. You have known the Lord for many years and served Him faithfully through your church, occupation, or ministry. What more do you have to learn about forgiveness? Chances are, plenty!

I, too, was in the ministry of our Lord Jesus Christ, but I was filled with so much hurt and bitterness that I could hardly fulfill my duties. I am almost ashamed to confess this. Astonishingly, before the reprimand from Josif, my unforgiving spirit had not bothered me all that much. If you had reminded me of Jesus' words that we should "love one another" (John 13:35) or of that petition in the Lord's Prayer, "Forgive us our debts, as we also have forgiven our debtors" (Matt. 6:12), I would have replied, "Of course I know about that." I assumed that since nobody is perfect and we all sin in some measure every day, the bitterness in my heart was no worse than any other person's transgression. Moreover, I thought, God fully understood and sympathized with my particular circumstances. In other words, I rationalized my attitude and behavior.

But mercifully, the Holy Spirit spoke to me that day through Josif's words. To be honest, I had only told Josif of my problem because I thought I would get sympathy from a man I deeply respected and who I thought would be on my side. I expected him to put his arm on my shoulder and say, "RT, you are right to feel so angry! Tell me all about it. Get it out of your system."

I was surprised by Josif's compassionate but sober rebuke. He would not let me off the hook. "You must totally forgive them," he told me in his Romanian accent.

"I can't," I replied.

"You can, and you must," he insisted.

Unsatisfied with his response, I tried to continue. "I just remembered. There is more. What I didn't tell you…"

"RT," he interrupted, "you must totally forgive them. Release them, and you will be set free."

It was the hardest thing I had ever been asked to do. But it was also the greatest thing I had ever been asked to do.

PERSONAL REFLECTIONS

1. You may be experiencing the same feelings I did. Have you rehearsed a wrong so that you could gain a friend's or colleague's sympathy? How did your listener receive what you were saying? How did you feel afterward? Circle the words that best describe the result of the conversation.

Fulfilling	Hollow
Helpful	Pointless
Warm	Harmful
Pleasing	Diabolical
Conclusive	

2. Have you ever been "wounded" by a friend in a way that led to your spiritual healing? Recount the incident briefly and how it changed your life.

_____

_____

_____

_____

_____

THE RETURN OF ALL-ENCOMPASSING PEACE

After that day, I began to forgive those who had hurt me, and a peace came into my heart that I had not felt in years. It was wonderful. I had forgotten what peace felt like. I was setting those people free, forgiving them, and letting them "off the hook." However, if I allowed myself to think about "what those people did," I would get churned up inside. I would say to myself, *They are going to get away with this. This is not fair! They won't get caught. They won't be found out. Nobody will know. This is not right!* And the sweet peace of the Lord would leave again.

I noticed an interesting cycle: when I allowed the spirit of total forgiveness to reign in my heart, the peace would return. But when I would dwell with resentment on the likelihood that they would not get caught, the peace would leave.

I had to make an important decision: which do I prefer—the peace or the bitterness? I could not have it both ways.

PERSONAL REFLECTIONS

1. Which do you prefer—your "hard-earned" bitterness or the peace of God? Reflect a moment on which reigns most often in your heart, and give yourself a score on the next page.

←————————————————————————————→

1	5	10
I always feel bitter about something	Sometimes I am bitter	I always feel at peace, free of bitterness

2. When was the last time you felt genuine, all-encompassing peace? Is it a daily occurrence for you or far too infrequent? Explain.

_____

_____

_____

_____

_____

In my case, I began to see that my bitterness was not damaging anyone but myself. When we are bitter, we delude ourselves into thinking that those who have hurt us are more likely to be punished as long as we are set on revenge. We are afraid to let go of those feelings. After all, if we do not make plans to see that justice is done, how will justice be done? We make ourselves believe that it is up to *us* to keep the offense alive. This is a lie—the devil's lie.

> Do not take revenge, my friends, but leave room for God's wrath, for it is written: "It is mine to avenge; I will repay," says the Lord.
> —ROMANS 12:19

We only hurt ourselves when we dwell on what has happened to us and fantasize about what it will be like when "they" get punished. Most of all, we grieve the Holy Spirit of God, and this is why we lose our sense of peace.

Personal Reflections

1. Have you ever imagined how your "enemies" might meet their doom? What are the images that have run through your head? Write down one or two of your "revenge fantasies" so that you can bring them out in the open. Be specific about what you have thought.

_____

_____

_____

_____

_____

2. Now read Ephesians 4:30–32, and summarize it in your own words.

_____

_____

_____

_____

_____

THE JOURNEY BEGINS

I found that I had to daily commit to forgive those who hurt me and to forgive them totally. I, therefore, let them utterly off the hook and resigned myself to this knowledge:

- They won't get caught or found out.

- Nobody will ever know what they did.

- They will prosper and be blessed as if they had done no wrong.

What's more, I actually began to *will* this! I prayed for it to happen. I asked God to forgive them. But I have had to do this every day to keep the peace within my heart. Having been on both sides, I can tell you: the peace is better. The bitterness is not worth it.

PERSONAL REFLECTIONS

1. Can you envision yourself coming to a place where you actually pray for those who have hurt you most deeply? List the names of the people for whom you have the hardest time praying.

   _____

   _____

   _____

   _____

2. Are you willing to take a journey to forgiveness regarding each of these people? Circle one.

   Yes   No

3. Now write a prayer asking God to help you complete this journey.

   _____

   _____

   _____

   _____

   _____

   _____

   _____

   _____

CHAPTER 2

WHEN IT HURTS
TO FORGIVE

MANY PEOPLE WHO have read my book *Total Forgiveness* have been through far worse than what I have experienced. But I have come to believe that the only way to move beyond the hurt and go forward in life is through total forgiveness. This theme of total forgiveness is perhaps more crucially needed at this present moment than nearly any other teaching in the Bible. Whenever I preach the message of total forgiveness, there is a tremendous response. No sermon or theme I ever touch on comes close to the chord that is struck when I share on this subject. The response tells me that there is a terrific need for this message—even among Christians.

One reason is that too few of us were taught how to forgive when we were young. I never felt sufficiently bothered by the unforgiveness I was harboring in my heart even as an adult. I have read hundreds of sermons by the Puritans and the Reformers, but I cannot recall being told by them I must totally forgive or otherwise grieve the Holy Spirit. Godly though my own parents were, I cannot say that forgiveness was something I was consciously taught at home. Not a single mentor that I can recall emphasized this as a lifestyle. On the contrary, I can remember being told: "Treat them with contempt"; "Distance yourself from them"; "Give them a cold shoulder"; "Teach them a lesson"; "They must be punished"; or other suggestions of that sort.

Some people marvel that a doctrine that seems so obvious in Scripture could apparently lie dormant, untaught for hundreds of years. But this should cause those of us who are church leaders to repent, not only for neglecting to teach forgiveness, but also for not putting it into practice in our own lives. Had this teaching been the emphasis and lifestyle of all of us who are in church leadership, there might not have been the division, hurt, and strife that have characterized many Christian circles. Though these strivings may often be described as a doctrinal battle for truth, so often the veneer is paper-thin, and underneath lie the age-old jealousies, petty agendas, and sheer humanness that affect us all.

PERSONAL REFLECTIONS

1. When did you receive your first lesson on forgiveness, and by whom? Define forgiveness in your own words.

_____

_____

_____

_____

2. Relate your earliest experience with giving and receiving genuine forgiveness.

_____

_____

_____

_____

FORGIVING DIFFICULT THINGS

Because forgiving those who have severely hurt us can be a very difficult task—especially when trust is shattered—Michelle Nelson has chosen to speak of degrees, or different types, of forgiveness.[1] She has listed three categories:

1. Detached forgiveness—Where there is a reduction in negative feelings toward the offender, but no reconciliation takes place.

2. Limited forgiveness—Where there is a reduction in negative feelings toward the offender and the relationship is partially restored, though there is a decrease in the emotional intensity of the relationship.

3. Full forgiveness—Where there is a total cessation of negative feelings toward the offender, and the relationship is fully restored.

I have chosen to speak of "total forgiveness," if only because that is the expression my friend Josif Tson used with me. This forgiveness must happen in the heart, and when it does, peace emerges. What does matter is that the Holy Spirit is able to dwell in us *ungrieved*, able to be utterly Himself. The degree to which the Holy Spirit is Himself in us will be the degree to which we are like Jesus and carry out His teachings.

You may think it is impossible to forgive your unfaithful husband or wife, or your abusive parent. You may feel you cannot forgive what was done to your son or daughter.

How can we forgive the church leader who took advantage of his position and spiritually abused us? What about the person who lied to us or about us, or the person who believed those lies? The list of potential offenses is endless.

I received a heartrending letter from a couple who had heard me teach on the subject of total forgiveness a few years ago. They told me what their son-in-law had done to their daughter and grandchildren. It was an awful story. "Are you saying we must totally forgive our son-in-law?" they asked. That was a hard question to answer, but I had to tell them the truth: yes, they must learn to forgive. It is the only way they will ever find freedom and release from the offense.

I have received many other letters that describe everything from infidelity to incest to rape to lying and slander. It is enough to make me consider very carefully indeed what I preach and write in this book. People experience real pain when another person hurts them or someone they love.

PERSONAL REFLECTIONS

1. What types of offenses do you find hardest to forgive?

    Personal betrayal
    A loved one's forgetfulness/carelessness
    A loved one's anger
    Being overlooked
    Being cheated
    Offenses involving money
    Offenses involving your children
    Other: _____

2. Which offenses do you find easiest to forgive? List them below.

    _____

    _____

    _____

    _____

    _____

EMBRACING THE "SELFISHNESS" OF FORGIVING

At the foot of Jesus' cross no one seemed very sorry. There was no justice at His "trial"—if you could even call it that. A perverse glee filled the faces of the people who demanded His death: "'Crucify him!' they shouted" (Mark 15:13). Furthermore, "those who passed by hurled insults at him, shaking their heads and saying, 'So! You who are going to destroy the temple and build it in three days, come down from the cross and save yourself!'" (Mark 15:29–30).

What was Jesus' response? "Father, forgive them, for they do not know what they are doing" (Luke 23:34). This must be our response as well. The ultimate proof of total forgiveness takes place when we sincerely petition the Father to let those who have hurt us off the hook.

One Sunday I unexpectedly saw a person in one of our services who had seriously hurt one of our children. I noticed the person just before I was scheduled to preach. In a flash the Lord seemed to say to me, "You say you want to see a revival take place in this church. But what if the beginning of a mighty revival hinges on whether or not you totally forgive this person?"

I felt awful. I felt selfish. I felt trapped. But I had to make a decision on the spot as to whether or not I really wanted a revival in my church. I had to choose which meant more to me—getting even with someone who had hurt one of my children or receiving the blessing of the Spirit. I opted for the latter, but my prayer still had a "selfish" explanation. I did not want it on my conscience that I had held up the blessing of the Spirit when all around me other believers were earnestly praying for it.

The motivation to forgive often has a "selfish" explanation, for Jesus speaks to us in a way that gets our attention—if only by appealing to our self-interest: "Do not judge, or you too will be judged" (Matt. 7:1). One selfish motive for not judging others is to keep from being judged ourselves.

If a person's chief desire is for a greater anointing, and he is told that this anointing will come in proportion to the degree that he forgives others, he will be more motivated to forgive. I, for one, want a greater anointing. If you could have seen my deepest heart when Josif Tson counseled me with the words,

"You must totally forgive them," you might have discovered that I acquiesced because I wanted a greater blessing from God. So it is not entirely selfless when one tries to forgive.

PERSONAL REFLECTIONS

1. What goals do you have in life that are threatened by your unforgiveness? Are you "selfish" enough to choose the path of total forgiveness? Imagine you have lived your whole life already. Write two brief versions of your life's story below: one assuming your highest dreams were blocked by unforgiveness, and the other assuming you freely forgave and let God's highest purpose for you come to pass. How are the stories different?

Story 1.

_____

_____

_____

_____

_____

Story 2.

_____

_____

_____

_____

_____

2. If your life was flooded with forgiveness, how would you be a different person right now? Explain.

Now read Colossians 3:13 aloud. Pay attention to that last phrase, "as the Lord forgave you."

How has the Lord forgiven you? Unequivocally and unconditionally. Your sins will never be held against you, and nobody will even know what you did. "As far as the east is from the west, so far has he removed our transgressions from us" (Ps. 103:12). It therefore follows that you should not hold people responsible for what they have done to you. You should hold nothing against them, and you should not tell other people, not even your closest friends, what they did to you.

You might reply, "But you shared everything that had been done to you with Josif Tson." That is true. And I am so glad I did! But I was not being malicious; I was not planning to start a smear campaign against anyone. Granted, my attitude was not perfect—I was seeking sympathy, but mercifully I was corrected. Without Josif's confrontation, I am not sure how long I could have kept silent. I can only thank God that He sent this wise person to me before I destroyed myself and my ministry.

David must have felt like this. One time before he was made king, he was fully ready to take vengeance on Nabal, a man who had refused to help him in his time of need. But God sent Abigail—just in the nick of time—to appeal to David's common sense:

> David said to Abigail, "Praise be to the LORD, the God of Israel, who has sent you today to meet me. May you be blessed for your good judgment and for keeping me from bloodshed this day and from avenging myself with my own hands. Otherwise, as surely as the LORD, the God of Israel,

lives, who has kept me from harming you, if you had not come quickly to meet me, not one male belonging to Nabal would have been left alive by daybreak."

—1 SAMUEL 25:32–34

If you must tell another person what happened—because you can't contain the pain—tell only one, and choose someone who won't repeat it. I only hope that person will be as faithful to you as Josif was to me.

PERSONAL REFLECTIONS

1. Who in your life can be trusted to "steer you right" when you share a burden with them? Are your friends confident enough in the Lord to rebuke you when you need it? Or do you need to find someone who will talk straight to you? List, in order, the people to whom you would approach for "straight talk."

_____

_____

_____

_____

2. Do you speak honestly and frankly to friends seeking advice, even when your words might hurt them? What does the Bible mean when it says, "Faithful are the wounds of a friend" (Prov. 27:6, KJV)? Explain this scripture in your own words.

_____

_____

_____

_____

_____

CHAPTER 3

WHAT TOTAL FORGIVENESS IS NOT

THERE ARE MANY things forgiveness *is*, and we will get to that shortly, but first let's dispel some common notions by discussing what total forgiveness *is not*.

1. Total forgiveness *is not* approving of what the person did.

Jesus forgave the woman found in adultery, but He did not approve of what she did. He told her, "Leave your life of sin" (John 8:11).

We are to maintain a healthy respect and fear of God's justice and forgiveness: "But with you there is forgiveness; therefore you are feared" (Ps. 130:4). Just as God forgives people without approving of their sin, we also must learn that forgiving people does not imply an endorsement of their evil deeds.

PERSONAL REFLECTIONS

1. Have you ever been in a situation where you "forgave" someone in a way that condoned the person's behavior? How did you respond? What would true forgiveness have done?

17

_____

_____

_____

_____

_____

2. Total forgiveness *is not* excusing what the person did.

We do not cover for the sins of other people. We do not point to circumstances in an attempt to explain away their behavior. While it is true that "every person is worth understanding," as Dr. Clyde Narramore says, this does not include excusing his inappropriate behavior.

PERSONAL REFLECTIONS

1. Have you ever blamed your circumstances instead of asking for forgiveness? How much weight should you give circumstances when deciding if a person has done wrong? Explain your view, and give biblical support.

_____

_____

_____

_____

_____

3. Total forgiveness *is not* justifying what the person did.

To *justify* means to "make right or just." God will never call something that is evil "right," and He does not require us to do so.

When Moses prayed for the Israelite people, he did not offer a hint of justification for their behavior. (See Numbers 14:11–12.) Instead he pointed out to God that the Egyptians would not think very highly of God's power or name if they saw Him obliterate

His own people. While we are required to forgive, we should never attempt to make what is wrong look like it is right.

1. Have you heard people try to justify their actions even after they received forgiveness? Have you ever caught yourself doing this, too? How can you avoid this trap?

_____

_____

_____

_____

_____

4. Total forgiveness *is not* pardoning what the person did.

A pardon is a legal transaction that releases an offender from the consequences of his action, such as a penalty or a sentence. I know of a lady who was raped by a person from a Middle Eastern country. At the time of the rape, she did not know he was from overseas; she found this out after he was caught. In the meantime she became a Christian. The police wanted her to testify at his trial. She was told he could be sent back to his homeland, which would mean he could be executed (the legal penalty for rape in his country).

She turned to me for advice. I counseled her to testify against this man. She had already forgiven him, but though she did not want to get him into trouble, if she did not testify, he would likely do it again. By the time she took the witness stand, there was no bitterness left in her heart; she was able to merely describe what had happened. As a result, the man was sent back to his own country. We never heard what happened to the man after he was extradited, but the potential punishment that he faced did not have any bearing on the forgiveness that had been offered by his victim.

1. Have you ever been in a situation, perhaps a court case or a simple matter of disciplining a child, where you had the power to forgive *and* to pardon? What did you do? Explain your decision.

_____

_____

_____

_____

_____

5. Total forgiveness *is not* reconciliation.

Forgiveness and reconciliation are not always the same. Reconciliation requires the participation of two people. The person you forgive may not want to see or talk to you, or he or she may have passed away since the time of the offense. Moreover, you may not want to maintain a close relationship with the person you forgive.

Reconciliation implies a restoration of relationship after a quarrel. When a husband and wife totally forgive each other, it will usually mean reconciliation—but not always. The bitterness and the desire to punish the other person may be gone, but the wish to restore things to the way they were may not necessarily be so strong. If your spouse is unfaithful and sleeps with your best friend, both your marriage and your friendship will probably never be the same, no matter how genuine the forgiveness that is offered.

An injured person can forgive an offender without reconciliation. It is wonderful indeed if the relationship can be restored, but this must not be pressed in most cases. Some things can never be the same again. It takes two to reconcile, and there must be a total willingness on both parts.

As 2 Corinthians 5:19 tells us, God was in Christ, reconciling the world to Himself. But we still implore people on Christ's behalf: "Be reconciled to God" (v. 20). Why must we do this? Reconciliation doesn't really take place until both parties agree.

PERSONAL REFLECTIONS

1. Write about an incident when you were genuinely reconciled to someone after an offense.

_____

_____

_____

_____

_____

2. Is there anyone in your life with whom you want to be reconciled but can't? Explain who and why.

_____

_____

_____

_____

_____

6. Total forgiveness *is not* denying what the person did.

Denying that an offense took place is almost always unconscious. Some people, for various reasons, live in denial; they refuse to admit or come to terms with the reality of a bad situation. It is sometimes painful to face the facts, and at times denial seems to be an easy way out.

This almost always has negative consequences for our psychological well-being. Repression cannot remove the wound. Even when the pain is pushed down into the cellar of our subconscious mind, it will still come out one way or another, often causing high blood pressure, nervousness, irritability, or even a heart attack.

True forgiveness can only be offered after we have come to terms with reality—when we can admit, "This person actually did or said this to me."

PERSONAL REFLECTIONS

1. Tell about a real-life situation in which someone you know denied he was hurt when it was obvious that he had been. What was the result? Did denial help or hinder forgiveness in the short run? What were the long-term effects? Explain.

_____

_____

_____

_____

_____

7. Total forgiveness *is not* blindness to what happened.

Willful blindness is a conscious choice to pretend that a sin did not take place (whereas repression is usually unconscious and involuntary). Both are wrong and can be psychologically damaging. When we play such word games with ourselves, we can delay coming to terms with our own responsibility to forgive. Someone who is trying to forgive an offense, but is actually pretending that the event never happened, will eventually explode and become an offender himself—all because he was not being true to the pain the original offense had caused.

Read 1 Corinthians 13:5. Some people use this verse to justify their willful blindness. But keeping "no record of wrongs" does not mean that we must be blind to those wrongs. True forgiveness of a wrong does not pretend that no wrong is there. The wrong must be acknowledged. We cannot be blind to it. We should not pretend it didn't happen.

Sometimes, if the person who hurt or wounded us is an authority figure or perhaps known to be very "godly," we may say to ourselves, "I didn't see this. I didn't hear this. This could not have happened; therefore, it didn't." But the truth is, sometimes the people we admire the most can do the most hurtful things to us. And it is of no value to pretend we didn't see it happen.

Personal Reflections

1. Describe a time when someone you respected—perhaps a friend, boss, or minister—committed a wrong that was too big or too painful to acknowledge. Did you find yourself denying that it could be true, even for a moment? How did you come to grips with it in the end?

_____

_____

_____

_____

_____

8. Total forgiveness *is not* forgetting.

When someone says we must "forgive and forget," I understand what he means. He is equating true forgiveness with wiping the memory of the event from his mind. But literally to forget may not be realistic. It is usually impossible to forget meaningful events in our lives, whether positive or negative.

Love doesn't erase our memories. It is actually a demonstration of greater grace when we are fully aware of what occurred—and we still *choose* to forgive. God doesn't literally forget our sins. He *chooses* to overlook them. He knows full well what we have done—every sordid detail. But He chooses not to remember while not holding our sins against us. (See Hebrews 8:12.) That is precisely what we are to do; although we may not be able to forget, we can still choose not to dwell on offenses.

PERSONAL REFLECTIONS

1. How do you "forget" offenses? Describe what steps you take to put thoughts of hurt and revenge in their place.

_____

_____

_____

_____

_____

9. Total forgiveness *is not* refusing to take the wrong seriously.

Some people may think that in order to forgive they must dismiss a wrong or pass it off as inconsequential or insignificant. But that is only avoiding the problem. The greater victory for the one who does the forgiving is to face up to the seriousness—even the wickedness—of what happened and still forgive.

This is what God does. He doesn't say, "Come now, my dear, that's not too bad. I can easily wash this sin away." No. He sent His Son to die for our sins, and Christ's sacrificial death proves just how serious a problem sin is. God doesn't pass our sins off as inconsequential, yet He forgives—totally.

PERSONAL REFLECTIONS

1. How do you recognize the seriousness of the offense while still offering grace? Give an example from your own experience.

_____

_____

_____

_____

_____

10. Total forgiveness *is not* pretending we are not hurt.

It is ridiculous to think that we should have to keep a stiff upper lip when we have been injured by a spouse's infidelity...or betrayed...or molested...or unjustly criticized.

Jesus was obviously hurt when He was struck in the face by a high priest's official. He even asked the man, "Why did you strike me?" (John 18:23). After all, Jesus endured the cross and scorned, rather than denied, the shame (Heb. 12:2). And He was able to say, "Father, forgive them, for they do not know what they are doing" (Luke 23:34).

Personal Reflections

1. Have you tried to pass off an offense as unimportant? Why did you downplay the depth of the hurt you experienced?

_____

_____

_____

_____

_____

Pause and ask God to help you avoid these traps on the way to total forgiveness.

CHAPTER 4

WHAT TOTAL FORGIVENESS IS

NOW LET'S TAKE a look at what total forgiveness is.

1. Being aware of what someone has done and still forgiving him

Total forgiveness is achieved only when we acknowledge what was done without any denial or covering up—and still refuse to make the offender pay for his crime. Total forgiveness is painful. It hurts to think that the person is getting away with what he did and to know that nobody else will ever find out. But when we know fully what the person did, and accept in our hearts that he will be blessed without any consequences for his wrong, we cross over into a supernatural realm. We begin to be a little more like Jesus, to change into the image of Christ.

PERSONAL REFLECTIONS

1. What does it feel like to crossover into that supernatural realm of total forgiveness? Do you think you are there now?

_____

_____

_____

_____

2. Rank your "forgiveness quotient" on the chart below.

←————————————————————————→

1   10

I never forgive   I forgive unequivocally

3. Name specific ways you want to grow in this area of forgiveness.

_____

_____

_____

_____

_____

2. Choosing to keep no records of wrong

Love "keeps no record of wrongs" (1 Cor. 13:5). Why do we keep track of the times we are offended? To use them. To prove what happened. A husband may say to his wife in a moment of anger, "I'll remember that." She may say to him, "I will never forget this." Many marriages could be healed overnight if both parties would stop pointing a finger.

When we develop a lifestyle of total forgiveness, we learn to erase the wrong rather than file it away in our mental computer. When we do this all the time—as a lifestyle—we not only avoid bitterness, but we also eventually experience total forgiveness as a feeling—and it is a good feeling.

PERSONAL REFLECTIONS

1. Read Isaiah 58:9. Write a prayer asking God to help
   you stop keeping records of wrongs and to develop total
   forgiveness, according to His Word.

   _____

   _____

   _____

   _____

   _____

3. Refusing to punish

If we harbor the desire to see our enemies punished, we will
eventually lose the anointing of the Spirit. But when perfect
love—the love of Jesus and the fruit of the Holy Spirit—enters,
the desire for our enemies to be punished leaves. Total forgiveness is refusing to punish. It is refusing to cave in to the fear that
this person or those people won't get the punishment or rebuke
we think they deserve.

Vindication is God's prerogative alone. Deuteronomy 32:35
tells us, "It is mine to avenge; I will repay." This verse is even
cited twice in the New Testament (Rom. 12:19; Heb. 10:30).
Vindication is what God does best. He doesn't want our help.
So when we refuse to be instruments of punishment, God likes
that; it sets Him free to decide what should be done. But if we
maneuver our way into the process, He may well let us do what
we will; then neither divine vengeance nor true justice will be
carried out—only the fulfillment of our personal grudge.

It is important that we examine ourselves in this area. We
must ask, "How much of what I am about to say or do is just an
attempt to punish?" If punishment is our motive, we are about to
grieve the Holy Spirit, however much right may be on our side.

PERSONAL REFLECTIONS

1. If you have ever tried to "punish" someone, how did things go? Did you feel justice was served? Explain.

_____

_____

_____

_____

_____

2. Can you think of a recent incident in which you tried to punish anyone, even in a small way? If so, what was the outcome? Are you a habitual "punisher," or do you let people off the hook? Explain.

_____

_____

_____

_____

_____

4. Not telling what they did

Anyone who truly forgives does not gossip about his offender. Talking about how you have been wounded with the purpose of hurting your enemy's reputation or credibility is just a form of punishing them.

When I recall that total forgiveness is forgiving others as I have been forgiven, I remember:

- I won't be punished for my sins.

- Nobody will know about my sins, for all sins that are under the blood of Christ will not be exposed or held against me.

Therefore when I blurt out what someone else has done to me, I am apparently forgetting that God will not tell what I did to Him. He has forgiven me of much, and He won't tell anyone about it. So, when I tell on my enemy, I am showing contempt for my own forgiveness.

PERSONAL REFLECTIONS

1. Do you take lightly all that you have been forgiven? Think back to what you have done that required God's forgiveness. Which best describes your thoughts: "I haven't been so bad," or "I'm absolutely awful"? Write a prayer asking God to constantly remind you of the magnitude of His grace in your life, especially when you are asked to forgive.

_____

_____

_____

_____

_____

_____

_____

5. Being merciful

"Blessed are the merciful, for they will be shown mercy" (Matt. 5:7). The Bible says basically two things about God:

- He is merciful.
- He is just.

The heart of the gospel is related to these two characteristics. Because He is merciful, God does not want to punish us; because He is just, He must punish us because we have sinned

31

against Him. So how can both of these sides of God be satisfied simultaneously?

The answer is the crux of the gospel message: He sent His Son, Jesus Christ—the God-man—to die on the cross for us. "We all, like sheep, have gone astray, each of us has turned to his own way; and the LORD has laid on him the iniquity of us all" (Isa. 53:6). Because God punished Jesus for our sins, He can now be true to Himself and still be truly merciful to us.

When it comes to being merciful, this is our Lord's command: "Be merciful, just as your Father is merciful" (Luke 6:36). Mercy is the opposite of wrath or justice. One difference between grace and mercy is that grace is getting what we don't deserve (favor), and mercy is not getting what we do deserve (justice). So when we show mercy, we are withholding justice from those who have injured us, which is one aspect of godliness.

There is a fringe benefit for those of us who show mercy: we will also be shown mercy (Matt. 5:7). This again shows that total forgiveness is not devoid of self-interest. "The merciful man doeth good to his own soul" (Prov. 11:17, KJV).

PERSONAL REFLECTIONS

1. Relate a recent incident in which you showed mercy. How did it feel to withhold justice? Explain when you think it is appropriate to give mercy, or if it is to be bestowed randomly, as you feel at that moment of decision.

_____

_____

_____

_____

_____

_____

6. Graciousness

True forgiveness shows grace *and* mercy at the same time. There is an interesting Greek word, *epieikes*, which means "forbearance" or "tolerance." It is the opposite of being unduly rigorous and severely judging. The idea is: do not make a rigorous stand against your enemy even when you are clearly in the right.

In Philippians 4:5 this word is translated "gentleness." It comes down to our English word *graciousness*. It implies an exceedingly rare act of grace. It cuts right across a legalistic spirit, which is what comes naturally to most of us. This concept is quite threatening to those of us who don't suffer fools gladly, who feel that being inflexible for the truth is the ultimate virtue.

Jesus was gracious all the time. When a group of self-righteous religious leaders led a woman who was found in the act of adultery to Jesus, there was no question that sin had taken place. But what was our Lord's attitude? Graciousness. They wanted to see if He would throw the book at her.

> When they kept on questioning him, he straightened up and said to them, "If any one of you is without sin, let him be the first to throw a stone at her."
>
> —JOHN 8:7

After the accusers slipped away:

> Jesus straightened up and asked her, "Woman, where are they? Has no one condemned you?"
>
> "No one, sir," she said.
>
> "Then neither do I condemn you," Jesus declared. "Go now and leave your life of sin."
>
> —JOHN 8:10–11

In this case there was no question a sin had taken place. But our Lord's attitude was to be gracious.

Graciousness is withholding certain facts you know to be true, so as to leave your enemy's reputation unscathed. Graciousness is shown by what you *don't* say, even if what you could say would be true. Self-righteous people find it almost impossible to be gracious; they claim always to be after "the truth," no matter the cost. Total forgiveness sometimes means overlooking what you perceive to be the truth and not letting on about anything that could damage another person.

PERSONAL REFLECTIONS

1. Explain the difference between the facts and the truth. Do the obvious facts of a situation always represent the complete truth of a situation?

_____

_____

_____

_____

_____

_____

2. Discuss a time when someone refused to be gracious and instead went after "the truth" at any cost. How did that person's pursuit of "truth" affect him and those closest to him? Did it make the situation better or worse?

_____

_____

_____

_____

_____

_____

7. It is an inner condition.

Total forgiveness must take place in the heart. It is my experience that most people we must forgive do not believe they have done anything wrong at all, or if they know that they did something wrong, they believe it was justified. I would even go so far as to say that at least 90 percent of all the people I've ever had to forgive would be indignant at the thought that they had done something wrong. If you gave them a lie-detector test, they would honestly say that they had done nothing wrong—and they would pass the test with flying colors.

You can still have the inner victory, even if your enemy doesn't recognize the offense and doesn't want to reconcile. Jesus gave us an example on the cross.

> Jesus said, "Father, forgive them, for they do not know what they are doing." And they divided up his clothes by casting lots.
>
> —LUKE 23:34

If we wait until our enemies feel some guilt or shame for their words and actions, we will never forgive them!

PERSONAL REFLECTIONS

1. Do you have any "hanging relationships" where you feel you have been done wrong, but the person who "wronged" you does not know he did or does not care? How have you dealt with this up to now? How do you intend to deal with it from now on? Note two or three things that you will do immediately to improve this situation/relationship as best you can.

_____

_____

_____

_____

_____

8. It is the absence of bitterness.

Bitterness is an excessive desire for vengeance that comes from deep resentment. It heads the list of the things that grieves the Spirit of God. It became Esau's preoccupation. (See Genesis 27:41.) And it is one of the most frequent causes of people missing the grace of God. "See to it that no one misses the grace of God and that no bitter root grows up to cause trouble and defile many" (Heb. 12:15). Bitterness will manifest itself in many ways—short temper, high blood pressure, irritability, sleeplessness, obsession with getting even, depression, isolation, a constant negative perspective, and generally feeling unwell.

We must, therefore, begin to get rid of a bitter and unforgiving spirit; otherwise, the attempt to forgive will fail. The absence of bitterness allows the Holy Spirit to be Himself in us. This means that we will become like Jesus. When the Spirit is grieved, each of us is left to himself, and we will struggle with emotions ranging from anger to fear.

How can we be sure that there is no bitterness left in our hearts? Bitterness is gone when there is no desire to get even or punish the offender, when I do or say nothing that would hurt his reputation or future, and when I truly wish him well in all he seeks to do.

PERSONAL REFLECTIONS

1. Have you, like Esau, held grudges against anybody for long periods of time? How has this grudge affected your life, your other relationships, your work, your worship? Be specific in your explanation.

_____

_____

_____

_____

_____

2. Do you now wish those people well, or is there more work to be done in your heart?

_____

_____

_____

_____

9. Forgiving God

Although we often do not see it at first—and for some it takes a long time—all of our bitterness is ultimately traceable to a resentment of God. This may be an unconscious anger. Some "good" people would be horrified at the thought that they could be harboring bitterness toward God.

Why do we feel this way? Because deep in our hearts we believe that He is the one who allowed bad things to happen in our lives. Since He is all-powerful and all-knowing, couldn't He have prevented tragedies and offenses from happening? The Bible says:

> All things work together for good to them that love God, to them who are the called according to his purpose.
> —ROMANS 8:28, KJV

God does turn evil into blessing. He causes things to work together for good. God did not send His Son into the world to explain evil, but rather to save us from it and to exemplify a life of suffering.

As for all the unhappy things He has allowed to happen, we must affirm His justice. He is God. He knows exactly what He is doing—and why. For all of us who struggle with God's right to allow evil to exist in the world, there still must be a genuine forgiveness on our part, because any bitterness toward God grieves the Holy Spirit. We therefore must forgive Him—though He is not guilty—for allowing evil to touch our lives.

PERSONAL REFLECTIONS

1. If a child asked you to explain the presence of evil in the world, what would you say?

_____

_____

_____

_____

_____

2. Are you, or have you ever been, angry with God? Explain.

_____

_____

_____

_____

3. If you struggle with bitterness against God, write an honest, gut-level prayer asking Him to help you with your struggle.

_____

_____

_____

_____

_____

Total forgiveness also means forgiving ourselves, but I want to delve into that deeply important topic at greater length later in the book. First, let's look at how we know we have totally forgiven.

CHAPTER 5

Chapter 2

HOW TO KNOW WE HAVE
TOTALLY FORGIVEN

MANY PEOPLE HAVE asked me, "How do I know when I have totally forgiven someone?" They sometimes say, "I think I have forgiven my offender, but I'm not sure."

The truth is, for a long time I didn't know how to answer them. I began to wonder whether I had totally forgiven certain people who had hurt me. The question bothered me so much that I began to search for an answer.

I found it, unexpectedly, in the life of Joseph. We know the basic outlines of his story: his brothers conspired to kill him because they were jealous of the attention he got from their father. Instead of killing him, they sold him as a slave to the Ishmaelites. But God was with him, and he began to work in the house of Potiphar, the Egyptian officer to whom the Ishmaelites had sold him. He was such a valuable employee that he was put in charge of the entire household. But the Bible describes Joseph as "well-built and handsome," and some time later Potiphar's wife began to flirt with him. "Come to bed with me!" she pleaded, but he refused.

As the saying goes, "Hell hath no fury like a woman scorned."

She accused Joseph of rape. Potiphar had Joseph put in prison. Joseph was punished for doing the right thing!

This was the beginning of a period of preparation for Joseph. He didn't realize it at the time, but God had great plans for him. Dr. Martyn Lloyd-Jones, my predecessor at Westminster Chapel, used to say to me, "The worst thing that can happen to a man is to succeed before he is ready." God wanted to ensure that Joseph did not come out of prison and embark on the next phase of his life's work until he was ready. The Bible says:

> The Lord disciplines those he loves, and he punishes everyone he accepts as a son.
> —HEBREWS 12:6

PERSONAL REFLECTIONS

1. Recall a time in your life when you went through a period of "punishment" and discipline at God's hand. Describe one such period in your life.

_____

_____

_____

_____

_____

2. How did you get through the time of God's discipline?

_____

_____

_____

_____

_____

Joseph had much to be bitter about. His brothers had treated him with cruelty and disdain. Potiphar's wife had falsely accused him. Most maddening of all, God had apparently allowed all of these things to take place. Joseph had many "offenders" to forgive.

After some time passed, Joseph had company in prison—Pharaoh's cupbearer and baker. While there, each of them had a dream that Joseph offered to interpret. He predicted that the baker would be hanged in three days, but that the cupbearer would get his job back in the same span of time.

But a temptation too great—so it seemed—was handed to Joseph on a silver platter. He had barely finished telling the cupbearer that he would be restored to Pharaoh's favor when Joseph got too involved in his prophetic word:

> But when all goes well with you, remember me and show me kindness; mention me to Pharaoh and get me out of this prison. For I was forcibly carried off from the land of the Hebrews, and even here I have done nothing to deserve being put in a dungeon.
>
> —GENESIS 40:14–15

These words prove to us that Joseph needed to be delivered from bitterness and self-pity. First Corinthians 13:5, the same verse that says love "keeps no record of wrongs," also says that love "is not self-seeking." If we are walking in love, we will not play the manipulator when it comes to promoting ourselves; we will let God promote us in His timing. Joseph was full of self-pity. He says so: "I have done nothing to deserve being put in a dungeon" (Gen. 40:15). At that point in time, Joseph had not yet forgiven his brothers, Potiphar's wife, or God.

PERSONAL REFLECTIONS

1. Recall a period of preparation in your life. What was your attitude during this time? How did your attitude affect the length of time?

_____

_____

_____

_____

_____

_____

2. When did you realize that the attitude of your heart
   was not right with God? Explain.

_____

_____

_____

_____

_____

LESSONS ON TOTAL FORGIVENESS

When Joseph's dreams finally came to pass, he was a changed man.
There was no bitterness. There were no grudges. Something
had happened to him during those final two years in prison.
When his brothers came to Egypt begging for food and stood
before Joseph, the new prime minister, Joseph wept. Filled with
love, he demonstrated total forgiveness.

What lessons about total forgiveness can the example of
Joseph teach us?

1. Do not let anyone know what someone said about you or did to you.

To ensure privacy, Joseph cried out, "Have everyone leave
my presence!" (Gen. 45:1). He waited to reveal his identity
until there was no one in the room except his brothers. Why
did Joseph make everyone else leave? Because he did not want

42

a single person in Egypt to know what his brothers had done to him twenty-two years before.

This is precisely how you and I are forgiven: "As far as the east is from the west, so far has he removed our transgressions from us" (Ps. 103:12). Our sins are "wiped out" (Acts 3:19). It is as though our sins don't exist anymore—they are gone! And God will not reveal what He knows. There are a lot of things God knows about me that I wouldn't want anyone else to know. He has enough on me to bury me! But you will never know any of it because God won't tell.

We all have skeletons in our closets; some are known to others, many are unknown. It is comforting to know that God freely and totally forgives all of our sins and will never tell what He knows. That is the way Joseph forgave, and that is why we are urged, "Be kind and compassionate to one another, forgiving each other, just as in Christ God forgave you" (Eph. 4:32).

PERSONAL REFLECTIONS

1. Has anyone "forgiven" you, then betrayed your trust with what they knew about you? What did it do to your reputation? Your emotional life? Your relationship with that person?

_____

_____

_____

_____

_____

_____

2. Have you made the mistake of sharing secrets about people you had forgiven? When did you realize you were wrong, and what did you do about it?

_____

_____

_____

_____

_____

_____

3. Do you find it difficult to stop talking about offenses
   you have suffered?

⟵——————————————————————————⟶

1	5	10
I never talk about them	I sometimes talk about them	I always look for opportunities to talk about them

4. What can you do to improve immediately in this area?

_____

_____

_____

_____

_____

2. Do not allow anyone to be afraid of you or intimidated by you.

Joseph revealed his identity to his brothers with tears and compassion. The last thing he wanted was for them to fear him. When we have not totally forgiven those who hurt us, it gives us a bit of pleasure to realize that they are afraid or intimidated. If someone who has hurt us—and knows it—freezes in anxiety when they see us approach, we may say to ourselves, "Good! They should be afraid of me!" But that only shows that there is still bitterness in our hearts.

Our insecurity is what causes us to want people to stand in awe of us. We become pretentious; we try to keep other people from knowing who we really are and what we are really like. Sometimes I think the most attractive thing about Jesus as a man was His unpretentiousness. Jesus did not try to create an "aura of mystique"; even common people could relate to him.

Joseph had ascended as high as one could get in power and prestige. Had he so desired, he could have made his brothers fall at his feet in fear and reverence. He could have reminded them of his dreams and their disbelief. He could have even said one of the favorite phrases of human beings everywhere: "I told you so."

But instead Joseph said, "Come close to me." He wanted them to feel no fear in his presence. He wanted to be loved rather than admired.

Paul said, "For you did not receive a spirit that makes you a slave again to fear, but you received the Spirit of sonship. And by him we cry, 'Abba, Father'" (Rom. 8:15). Once He has forgiven us, God does not want us to be afraid of Him. What Joseph wanted his brothers to feel is what Jesus wants us to feel about Himself and the Father. "Anyone who has seen me has seen the Father," said Jesus (John 14:9). Jesus wants to put us at ease in His presence.

"There is no fear in love" (1 John 4:18). Joseph did not want his brothers to be afraid, and when we have totally forgiven our offenders, we will not want them to be afraid either.

PERSONAL REFLECTIONS

1. Have you ever trembled in the presence of someone you wronged? Were they able to put you at ease?

_____

_____

_____

_____

_____

2. How do you make yourself accessible and real to people who wronged you? Explain.

_____

_____

_____

_____

_____

3. We will want them to forgive themselves and not feel guilty.

Joseph told his brothers, "And now, do not be distressed and do not be angry with yourselves for selling me here" (Gen. 45:5). He was not about to send them on a guilt trip; he knew that they felt guilty enough (Gen. 42:21).

Sometimes we say, in effect, "I forgive you for what you did, but I hope you feel bad about it." This shows we still want to see that person punished. Those of us who are always sending people on guilt trips almost certainly have a big problem ourselves with a sense of guilt. Because we haven't sorted out our own guilt issues, we want to make sure others wallow in the mire of guilty feelings with us.

I sometimes think guilt is one of the most painful feelings in the world. My own greatest pain over the years has been guilt—and being reminded of my own failure, especially as a parent. If someone wanted to hurt me—to really and truly make me feel awful—all they would have to do is ask, "How much time did you spend with your kids in those critical years as they were growing up?" I am grateful that my children have totally forgiven me for my sins as a parent, but I still struggle with feelings of guilt for the mistakes that I made.

Joseph wanted to set his brothers free. He did not want them to blame or be angry with themselves; he wanted them to forgive themselves. To ease their minds, Joseph gave an explanation for his suffering: "It was to save lives that God sent me ahead of you" (Gen. 45:5). God does that with us as well; He wants to make it easy for us to forgive ourselves. That is partly why He gave us what is possibly Paul's most astonishing promise:

> And we know that all things work together for good to them that love God, to them who are the called according to his purpose.
>
> —ROMANS 8:28, KJV

God doesn't want us to continue to feel guilty, so He says, "Just wait and see. I will cause everything to work together for good to such an extent that you will be tempted to say that even the bad things that happened were good and right."

This then is total forgiveness: not wanting our offenders to feel guilty or upset with themselves for what they did, and showing them that there is a reason God let it happen.

PERSONAL REFLECTIONS

1. What was the most astonishing experience you have had of something good coming from bad circumstances?

_____

_____

_____

_____

_____

2. Do you believe good can come from any bad event, or are some too awful? How does your view square with Romans 8:28?

_____

_____

_____

---

3. What circumstance is there in your life now that you want to turn from bad to good? Write a prayer thanking God for this promise and asking Him to fulfill it speedily.

---

4. Write a prayer asking God to increase the evidence in your life that you have been forgiven.

Is it possible to totally forgive? I declare, yes! Next, let's look at more evidences that we have embarked on this road of forgiveness.

CHAPTER 6

HELPING OTHERS FEEL FORGIVEN

IN OUR QUEST for total forgiveness, we need to help others know that we have forgiven them without reservation. We will take a closer look at this further evidence.

1. We will let them save face.

Joseph told his brothers something that is, without doubt, the most magnanimous, gracious, and emancipating statement he had made so far: "You didn't do this to me; God did."

> But God sent me ahead of you to preserve for you a remnant on earth and to save your lives by a great deliverance. So then, it was not you who sent me here, but God. He made me father to Pharaoh, lord of his entire household and ruler of all Egypt.
>
> —GENESIS 45:7–8

This is as good as it gets. When we can forgive like that, we're there. We have achieved total forgiveness. Saving face means preserving one's dignity and self-esteem. It provides a rationale that enables what they did to look good rather than bad. Or it may mean hiding a person's error from people so they won't be embarrassed.

You can make a friend for life by letting someone save face. God lets us save face by causing our past (however foolish) to work out for our good. God did send Joseph to Egypt with a purpose in mind. Joseph was not one whit better than a single one of his brothers, and he was not about to act like it. He simply felt grateful to see them again and grateful to God for everything that he had been brought through. The preparation, the false accusations, all of the lies, pain, and suffering were worth it.

It is reminiscent of Jesus' words to His disciples: "A woman giving birth to a child has pain because her time has come; but when her baby is born she forgets the anguish because of her joy that a child is born into the world. So with you: Now is your time of grief, but I will see you again and you will rejoice, and no one will take away your joy" (John 16:21–22).

When we let people save face we are doing what is right and just, not being merely magnanimous and gracious.

PERSONAL REFLECTIONS

1. When was the last time someone let you save face to escape monumental embarrassment? Explain the circumstance.

_____

_____

_____

_____

_____

How did it make you feel toward that person? Grateful? Wary? Astonished? Explain.

_____

_____

_____

_____

_____

2. What are ways that you can help co-workers, family members, or friends to save face on a daily basis? Write a plan of action.

_____

_____

_____

_____

_____

2. We will protect them from their greatest fear.

No sooner had Joseph's brothers absorbed the good news than they experienced the greatest fear of all: they would have to return to Canaan and tell their father the truth of what they did. You can be sure that they'd rather have died than face their aged father with the truth behind that bloodstained coat of many colors that had been laid before him.

Joseph, knowing their guilt and dread, had already anticipated this problem and was a step ahead of them. He knew that his forgiveness of what they had done was utterly worthless to them if they had to tell the whole truth to their father. So Joseph told them exactly what to say and what not to say to Jacob. His direction was worded carefully, and it told their father all of the truth that he needed to know. (See Genesis 45:9–13.)

Sin that is under the blood of our sovereign Redeemer does not need to be confessed to anyone but God. If you need to share your situation with one other person for therapeutic purposes, fine. But you should not involve an innocent person by unloading information on him that he can easily live without. Instead, confess your sin to God.

> Against you, you only, have I sinned
> and done what is evil in your sight,
> so that you are proved right when you speak
> and justified when you judge.
>
> —PSALM 51:4

You may think the brothers should have confessed their sin to their father. Really? Wouldn't that have given Jacob an even greater problem—having to struggle with the regret of lost years with Joseph and with bitterness against his other sons?

When I consider the fact that our Lord Jesus Christ knows all about my sin but promises to keep what He has forgiven a carefully guarded secret, it increases my gratitude to Him. Many of us have one single greatest fear. I know I do. I know what I would fear the most—were it to be told. But God does not blackmail us. To hold another person in perpetual fear by threatening, "I'll tell on you," will quickly bring down the wrath of God. When I ponder the sins for which I have been forgiven, it is enough to shut my mouth for the rest of my life.

PERSONAL REFLECTIONS

1. How have you gone the extra mile and protected someone from his greatest fear?

   _____

   _____

   _____

   _____

   _____

   _____

2. Think about your greatest fear, your ugliest secret.
   Explain how this fear affects you today, and write a
   prayer asking God to free you from it and give you rest
   from your past.

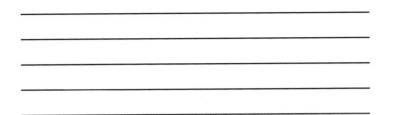

3. It is a lifelong commitment.

Making a lifelong commitment to total forgiveness means that you keep on doing it—for as long as you live. It isn't enough to forgive today and return to the offense tomorrow. I heard of a person whose wife said, "I thought you forgave me." He replied, "That was yesterday." Total forgiveness is a lifelong commitment, and you may need to practice it every single day of your life until you die. No one said it would be easy.

Seventeen years after reuniting with his long-lost son, Jacob died. Joseph's brothers suddenly panicked. They were terrified that Joseph's forgiveness would last only as long as their aged patriarch was still alive. "When Joseph's brothers saw that their father was dead, they said, 'What if Joseph holds a grudge against us and pays us back for all the wrongs we did to him?'" (Gen. 50:15).

Because of their fear, they concocted a story:

> So they sent word to Joseph, saying, "Your father left these instructions before he died: 'This is what you are to say to Joseph: I ask you to forgive your brothers the sins and the wrongs they committed in treating you so badly.' Now please forgive the sins of the servants of the God of your father."
> —Genesis 50:16–17

When Joseph heard this message, he wept. He could not believe that his brothers doubted him.

> But Joseph said to them, "Don't be afraid. Am I in the place of God? You intended to harm me, but God intended it for good to accomplish what is now being done, the saving

of many lives. So then, don't be afraid. I will provide for you and your children." And he reassured them and spoke kindly to them.

—GENESIS 50:19–21

What Joseph had done seventeen years before still held good; he was prepared to care for his brothers indefinitely. "I forgave you then, and I forgive you now," he was saying to them.

In my own case the temptation to return to bitterness was very real. I would concoct conversations in my head, imagining what I might say or recalling what had taken place, and I would get churned up. But if I took a step back and observed the situation from a distance, I could see the folly of such thinking. I had to keep on forgiving. Total forgiveness must go on and on and on.

If you are prepared to make a covenant to forgive—and to forgive totally—you must realize you will have to renew that covenant tomorrow. And it may be even harder to do tomorrow than it is today. It could even be harder next week—or next year. But this is a lifetime commitment.

PERSONAL REFLECTIONS

1. What are the easy days of forgiveness like? What about the hard days? Explain the ups and downs as you experience them in your life.

_____

_____

_____

_____

_____

2. What thoughts haunt you in the "down" times when revenge and bitterness seem so attractive? Be specific, and write them down.

_____

_____

_____

_____

3. Which scriptures have helped you in tough times when forgiveness seemed impossible?

_____

_____

_____

_____

4. What benefits have you experienced from long-term forgiveness?

_____

_____

_____

_____

5. Pretend you are giving advice to someone younger than you. What advice would you give him about forgiveness? Write it in your own words.

_____

_____

_____

_____

4. We will pray for them to be blessed.

Total forgiveness involves praying for God's blessings to rain on the lives of your offenders. "But I tell you: Love your enemies and pray for those who persecute you" (Matt. 5:44). When you do this as Jesus intends it, you are being set free indeed.

You don't pray, "God, deal with them. Get them for what they did to me." And neither is it enough to say, "Father, I commend them to You." That's a cop-out. You must pray that they receive total forgiveness, just as you want it for yourself. You pray that they will be dealt with as you want God to deal with you. (See Matthew 7:12.)

Praying like this, to quote John Calvin, "is exceedingly difficult." To me the greatest inspiration to live in this manner is found in the life—and death—of Stephen. While his enemies threw stones at him, he prayed—seconds before his last breath—"Lord, do not hold this sin against them" (Acts 7:60). And therein lies the secret to his unusual anointing.

If you are still asking, "How can I know that I have totally forgiven my enemy?" I answer, "Walking out these seven principles is as near as you can come to exhibiting total forgiveness."

PERSONAL REFLECTIONS

1. Fashion a prayer in your own words asking God to help you forgive and keep forgiving.

CHAPTER 7

THE LORD'S PRAYER AND FORGIVENESS

I SUPPOSE THAT the fifth petition of the Lord's Prayer, "Forgive us our debts as we also have forgiven our debtors," has made liars out of more people than any other line in human history. But Jesus clearly regarded this as the most important petition in His prayer. It is a plea for forgiveness from God. But then comes the following line (or possibly the big lie): "as we also have forgiven our debtors." That is a claim that we have already forgiven those who hurt us.

BEING HONEST WITH OURSELVES ABOUT BITTERNESS

Here's an even harder truth: John says, "If we claim to have fellowship with him yet walk in the darkness, we lie and do not live by the truth" (1 John 1:6). One way we walk in darkness is by holding bitterness in our hearts toward others—bitterness that creates confusion in our minds and oppression in our hearts. You may say, "Oh, but I am having fellowship with God." No, you're not. You just claim you are having fellowship with God if there is

57

bitterness in your heart. And if we claim to have fellowship with God but walk in darkness, we lie.

Walking in darkness is the consequence of unforgiveness. When I don't forgive, I might spend hours a day in prayer, but I am not having genuine fellowship with God. If I can't forgive the person who hurt someone dear to me, I am walking in darkness. If I can't forgive the person who lied about me to others, I have lost my intimate relationship with the Father. I can even continue to preach, and people may even say, "Oh, what a wonderful sermon! You must be so close to God!" I can sing praises to the Lord with my hands in the air, and you may say, "Oh, look at how RT is worshiping the Lord!" I could put on such an act that you would think that I am the holiest person in the church. But if I have bitterness inside or am holding a grudge against someone else, I am a liar. I cannot walk in the light when I am really in darkness.

There are two things Jesus takes for granted in the Lord's Prayer: that people have hurt us, and that we ourselves will need to be forgiven. We have all come short of God's glory, and often other people come short of treating us with the dignity, love, and respect that we would like. We have hurt God, and we want to be let off the hook; people have hurt us, and we must let them off the hook.

In what ways have you been hurt by other people? Perhaps you have been discredited or dishonored; maybe you have been disappointed that people could be so ungrateful. You may have been lied about or taken advantage of; people may not have been very appreciative; they may have been disloyal. In any case, our bitterness—however justified we feel in nurturing it—will hurt us more than anyone. It robs us of the pleasure and privilege of walking in the light with God with a pure heart. There should be nothing more important to us than our relationship with God. The apostle John said, "And our fellowship is with the Father and with his Son, Jesus Christ" (1 John 1:3). Do you put a high value on your times of fellowship with the Father? If you choose to withhold forgiveness from others, you are not putting a high enough value on something that should mean everything to you.

PERSONAL REFLECTIONS

1. List the people in your life who have *not* disappointed you at one time or another.

_____

_____

_____

_____

2. How long is the list? Did even one person make it? Now talk about how you have learned to deal with disappointments. Be honest. Don't just write the answer you wish were true. Write the actual facts.

_____

_____

_____

_____

3. What does it feel like to walk in darkness? Have you ever felt your prayers were being "blocked" by unforgiveness? How have you gotten out of "darkness" in the past?

_____

_____

_____

_____

WHEN PEOPLE DON'T MEAN TO HURT US

There is more than one kind of wound that causes hurt and pain. In some cases, people disappoint you by doing things they think are necessary. They don't intend to hurt you, but they do. As a parent or church leader, you sometimes do this—you must make a decision and then say, "I'm sorry, but this is the way it has to be."

People in my life have made these kinds of decisions. Even though wounding me was not their motive, they knew their decisions would hurt me, and they did. In these cases, the offense is not an outright sin you must forgive, but you are hurt nonetheless.

On the other hand, there are people in our world whose actions are called "sin." And again, there is more than one kind of such sin. There are sins that are not willfully committed, but nonetheless are done without any sensitivity toward the feelings of others. A person can be so full of himself—due to his own anger or ambition—that he hurts other people without realizing it. Never forget that you might have hurt others unwittingly; we all sin every day, and we therefore should pray daily for those we have hurt without even knowing it.

We must learn to foster a spirit of sensitivity to those around us. The more sensitive I am to the Holy Spirit, the more aware I will be of people around me who are in pain. Remember the words written about Jesus: "A bruised reed he will not break" (Matt. 12:20). I want to treat every single person I meet in that manner, but I fear I do not always do that. So there is one kind of sin where the offenders are not malicious, they are not hateful, and their motive is not to hurt, but they still sin through their insensitivity to others.

Personal Reflections

1. Talk about a time when someone unintentionally hurt you. How did you resolve it in your heart?

_____

_____

_____

_____

2. In what way do you consider yourself to be a sensitive person? What are the benefits and drawbacks of being sensitive? Of being insensitive?

_____

_____

_____

_____

Rate yourself on a sensitivity scale.

$\longleftarrow$ ————————————————— $\longrightarrow$

1   10

Totally insensitive to others   Overly sensitive to others

3. How can you mature in this area? Explain.

_____

_____

_____

_____

HURT CAUSED BY SINS KNOWINGLY COMMITTED

There are also sins that are willfully committed. Some people do wicked things with their eyes wide open, and these people surely have to know they have done something wrong. You may say, "Do I have to forgive even that?" The answer is yes.

There is a wonderful consolation, however: the greater the sin you must forgive, the greater the measure of the Spirit that will come to you. So if you have an extremely difficult situation on your hands, and you say, "I can't forgive this," you may not realize at first that there, handed to you on a silver platter, is an opportunity to receive a measure of anointing that someone else might not ever get! Consider it a challenge and an opportunity;

take it with both hands. Welcome the opportunity to forgive the deepest hurt, the greatest injustice, and remember that a greater anointing is waiting for you.

PERSONAL REFLECTIONS

1. What is the biggest injustice you have ever had to forgive? How long did it take for you to "perfect" forgiveness, or are you still working on it?

_____

_____

_____

_____

_____

2. What have been the rewards in your life? What makes you keep going for it?

_____

_____

_____

_____

_____

RESENTMENT AND REVENGE

God condemns an unforgiving spirit. "If you do not forgive men their sins, your Father will not forgive your sins," Jesus said. There are three reasons why.

1. It shows an indifference to the greatest thing God did.

This "greatest thing" was God sending His Son to die on the cross for our sins. To be forgiven is the most wonderful thing in the world. But in order to forgive us, God paid a severe price. God did for us what we did not deserve. He therefore wants us to pass this on to others who don't deserve it.

2. We interrupt God's purpose in the world: reconciliation.

God has given the ministry of reconciliation to us, and He wants it to continue. When we are forgiven, He wants us to pass it on. When we interrupt that, He doesn't like it at all.

3. God hates ingratitude.

God knows the sins for which He has forgiven us, and He loves a grateful response. If we turn around and say, "I can't forgive that person for what he has done," like the wicked servant in Matthew 18, God is displeased. He hates ingratitude.

Having an unforgiving spirit usually begins with resentment. A person becomes preoccupied with hate and self-pity. He can't come to terms with the possibility that the person who committed such an awful act against him will not get caught. He wants the offender exposed.

Resentment leads to going over and over again in your mind what the offender did, recounting and reliving exactly what happened. You should not dwell on the incident...or even think about it. It will not bring you any relief or release; instead, it will cause you to become even more churned up.

All of this leads to wanting to get even, to take revenge. You become determined to make your offender pay, not unlike the servant who had been forgiven a great debt, but who still said, "Pay me back, pay me back!" He had been forgiven, but he couldn't pass that forgiveness on to another.

We may also seek our revenge by hurting that person's reputation, by keeping others from thinking well of him. We may even take the punishment further and administer justice personally, trying to mete out the most severe penalty available to us. Never mind that God says, "Vengeance is mine!" Never mind that God says, "This is something that only I do." If we do it—let me make you a promise, it will only be one-tenth of what

God would have done. If you and I can't wait on God's timing and His manner, and we say, "I'm going to make sure justice is carried out," God says, "You're on your own."

PERSONAL REFLECTIONS

1. What do you think God means when He says vengeance is His? Do you think He will give out harsh justice or grant mercy to your enemies? Does it matter? Explain.

_____

_____

_____

_____

_____

THE CONSEQUENCES OF AN UNFORGIVING SPIRIT

1. The Holy Spirit is grieved.

"And do not grieve the Holy Spirit of God, with whom you were sealed for the day of redemption" (Eph. 4:30). Your relationship with the Holy Spirit should be one of the most important priorities in your life. When the Holy Spirit is grieved, it causes a distortion in our thinking. The ungrieved Spirit is what enables us to cope. I would not be able to do my job if the Holy Spirit were permanently grieved with me. I would not be able to function or think clearly. If I have spoken a sharp word to my wife, Louise, or to my kids or someone around me, or if I have harbored feelings of resentment, trying to prepare a sermon is impossible. Why? My attitude grieves the Spirit.

It is no different for you. You want to be at your best, whether working with computers; being a teacher, lawyer, doctor, or nurse; or simply typing a letter. You do not want the Holy Spirit to be upset with you. Let's not forget that immediately after Paul admonished us not to grieve the Spirit, he added:

> Get rid of all bitterness, rage and anger, brawling and slander, along with every form of malice. Be kind and compassionate to one another, forgiving each other, just as in Christ God forgave you.
>
> —EPHESIANS 4:31–32

2. You are left to yourself.

A refusal to forgive means that God stands back and lets you cope with your problems in your own strength. Not many people want to live that kind of life. Personally, I couldn't bear it. The Bible says the backslider is "filled with his own ways" (Prov. 14:14, KJV), so when one is left to oneself and to the flesh, those unthinkable capabilities toward sin in that person are given free reign. Not only that, but Satan is also able to get in. He will take advantage of us if he can. (See 2 Corinthians 2:11.) He will exploit that unforgiving spirit, play on your self-pity, and, worst of all, you may fancy that God is with you in this!

3. You force God to become your enemy.

> What causes fights and quarrels among you? Don't they come from your desires that battle within you? You want something but don't get it. You kill and covet, but you cannot have what you want. You quarrel and fight. You do not have, because you do not ask God. When you ask, you do not receive, because you ask with wrong motives, that you may spend what you get on your pleasures.
>
> You adulterous people, don't you know that friendship with the world is hatred toward God? Anyone who chooses to be a friend of the world becomes an enemy of God.
>
> —JAMES 4:1–4

The reason God treats you like an enemy is because, by not forgiving others, you are really saying, "God, move over; I want to do Your job!" You crown yourself judge, jury, and executioner, and you presume to take God's place.

4. You lose the potential of your anointing.

When you will not forgive, the anointing God may have given to you is lifted, and you will become like an empty shell. You may be able to continue for a while, because the gifts of God are irrevocable. (See Romans 11:29.) Even King Saul prophesied for a while after the Spirit left him, but eventually he lost everything.

Next to my salvation, I regard the anointing as the most precious thing I have on this earth. I do not want to lose the anointing of God. We may flourish for a while; the momentum of other gifts in us may make us think we still have the anointing we enjoyed yesterday. But mark this down: bearing a grudge and trying to punish and get even will cut off your anointing. The loss will become apparent sooner or later—unless you choose to forgive and forgive totally.

5. We risk losing our heavenly reward.

Some may go to heaven without a reward. "If what he has built survives, he will receive his reward. If it is burned up, he will suffer loss; he himself will be saved, but only as one escaping through the flames" (1 Cor. 3:14–15).

Why did Jesus give this word in His model prayer? He did it to motivate us. It's a warning we all must heed. And if a person who is not a Christian can be motivated to forgive, even if only in a limited way, how much more should we as Christians be motivated by the Holy Spirit to forgive—totally?

PERSONAL REFLECTIONS

1. Do you sense the Holy Spirit is grieved with you for any reason? Have you become an enemy of God? Are you at risk of losing the potential of your anointing or your heavenly reward? Take a moment to meditate on

the Lord, with an open heart toward making things right. When you are ready, write a prayer that sums up what is in your heart. Ask for forgiveness if you need to.

_____

_____

_____

_____

_____

CHAPTER 8

PLAYING GOD

WHEN JESUS SAID, "Be perfect, therefore, as your heavenly Father is perfect" (Matt. 5:48), He was setting the stage for a higher level of perfection than many Christians have even thought to strive for. What we see in Jesus' words, "Do not judge, or you too will be judged," is an example of this level of maturity that allows us to have a true intimacy with God and a greater anointing.

Judging someone else is actually uncalled-for criticism. That's what Jesus means by judging. When Jesus says, "Do not judge," He is not telling us to ignore what is wrong. He is saying not to administer any uncalled-for criticism; that is, criticism that is unfair or unjustified.

One acrostic that I have found helpful is built on the word *NEED*. When speaking to or about another person, ask yourself if what you are about to say will meet his needs:

Necessary—Is it necessary to say this?

Encourage—Will this encourage him? Will it make him feel better?

Edify—Will it edify? Will what you say build him up and make him stronger?

Dignify—Will it dignify that person? Jesus treated other people with a sense of dignity.

Criticism that is either unfair or unjust, even if it is true, should not be uttered. The fact that what you would say is true does not necessarily make it right to say. Often Satan's accusations are true; he is an expert at being a judge. He is even called "the accuser of our brothers" (Rev. 12:10). You may be pointing your finger and speaking words of truth, but you may unwittingly be an instrument of the devil as you speak.

For years I have read Luke 6:37 every day; it says, "Do not judge, and you will not be judged." Why have I chosen this particular verse to focus on? Because judging is probably my greatest weakness.

Judging other people is almost always counterproductive. When I judge someone else I may be thinking, *What I want to do is change this person, straighten this person out.* But it has the opposite effect almost every time! Sooner or later it will backfire. The other person will become offended, and the situation is not resolved.

PERSONAL REFLECTIONS

1. Have you ever judged someone wrongly? Explain the situation and the result.

_____

_____

_____

_____

_____

2. Have you been judged wrongly? How did it feel? Did it help you along in your faith walk or stall you? Explain.

_____

_____

BEING CRITICAL OF OTHERS

Being judged is painful, whether or not the accusation is true. Jesus has given us a pragmatic reason not to judge. If you don't like being judged yourself, then stop judging other people. Avoid dishing out criticism, and you will escape being criticized. This immediately appeals to our self-interest.

God could throw the book at me at any time. But He won't—that is, unless He sees me pointing my finger at somebody else. Then God will say, "Sorry about this, RT, but I must step in and deal with you. You should know better." God Himself will see that I am judged if I judge others.

It is so easy to criticize. You don't need to read a book on how to develop a pointing finger. You don't need more education, a higher IQ, or a lot of experience to get good at it, and judging is certainly no sign you are more spiritual. It has often been said that a little bit of learning is a dangerous thing. Sometimes a little bit of spirituality is a dangerous thing as well, because one may be just spiritual enough to see what is wrong in others—and to point the finger. The true test of spirituality is being able not to point the finger!

You may say, "Well, I have to say something, or nobody else will!" So what if no one else does? The person you are judging likely doesn't want to hear it, so we are not really helping anyway. When they are judged, they usually will feel worse but not change their behavior. God's Word is a practical command. "Stop it!" He says.

> If you do away with the yoke of oppression, with *the pointing finger* and malicious talk, and if you spend yourselves on behalf of the hungry and satisfy the needs of the oppressed, then your light will rise in the darkness, and your night will become like the noonday.
> —ISAIAH 58:9–10, EMPHASIS ADDED

71

Consider the atmosphere you live in when it is devoid of criticism. How pleasant it is when we all live in harmony! (See Psalm 133:1.) It is so sweet and so good. Now consider the pain that follows when someone is critical of you. If you don't like being criticized, don't criticize others!

PERSONAL REFLECTIONS

1. Describe a good atmosphere you have experienced where there was no ungodly criticism.

_____

_____

_____

_____

_____

2. How can you foster that atmosphere at work? At home? At church?

_____

_____

_____

_____

_____

JUDGING IS GOD'S PREROGATIVE

The word *godliness* means "being like God," and there are certain aspects of God's character that He commands us to imitate. For example, we are commanded to live holy lives: "Be holy, because I am holy" (1 Pet. 1:16). We are commanded to show mercy to our neighbors: "Be merciful, just as your Father is merciful" (Luke 6:36). God wants us to walk in integrity. He wants us to walk in truth and sincerity. But there is an aspect of the character of God where there is no trespassing allowed, and the moment we begin to point our fingers at other people, we are on it—we are sinning. That aspect is being a judge.

If you and I are foolish enough to administer uncalled-for criticism, we should remember three things:

- God is listening.
- He knows the truth about us.
- He is ruthlessly fair.

As Malachi says:

> Then those who feared the LORD talked with each other, and the LORD listened and heard. A scroll of remembrance was written in his presence concerning those who feared the LORD and honored his name.
> —MALACHI 3:16

Never forget that God knows the truth about us! "Nothing in all creation is hidden from God's sight. Everything is uncovered and laid bare before the eyes of him to whom we must give account" (Heb. 4:13). How would you like it if, as you are pointing the finger at someone else, an angel from heaven showed up and said, "Stop! Here's what I know about you," and then he revealed your secret sins to the person you were judging? God could just do that. While you are busy pointing your finger, God may be looking down from heaven with the angels and saying, "I can't believe he would talk that way, because We know all about him!"

Here are two practical verses that we all would do well to consider:

> Do not pay attention to every word people say,
>   or you may hear your servant cursing you.
> —ECCLESIASTES 7:21

Do not revile the king even in your thoughts,
  or curse the rich in your bedroom,
because a bird of the air may carry your words,
  and a bird on the wing may report what you say.
                              —ECCLESIASTES 10:20

God has a way of exposing us just when we begin to think, *There is no way that could happen to me.* The Lord promises that equitable judgment will be administered. The word *equitable* means "fair" or "just." All of God's judgments are ruthlessly fair. At the judgment seat of Christ, before which we will all stand one day, for once in human history judgment will be fair.

Nearly every day we hear of the courts letting someone off, and we say to ourselves, "Where is the justice?" But God's justice is always fair. The question is, Will it occur here in this present life or in the life to come? Paul said:

For we must all appear before the judgment seat of Christ, that each one may receive what is due him for the things done while in the body, whether good or bad.
                              —2 CORINTHIANS 5:10

You, then, why do you judge your brother? Or why do you look down on your brother? For we will all stand before God's judgment seat.
                              —ROMANS 14:10

On the other hand, God does deal with people in this present life, especially if they are saved. In 1 Corinthians 11:30, Paul says, "That is why many among you are weak and sick, and a number of you have fallen asleep." God doesn't always wait for the final judgment to begin disciplining His children.

Perhaps you have said, "Whew, I got away with that!" Perhaps God has closed His eyes to it. That is possible, since He has not always dealt with us after our sins or rewarded us according to our iniquities (Ps. 103:10). On the other hand, it could be that God is so angry that He has decided to wait. Usually, the angrier

He is, the longer He waits.

God is not out to judge us because He enjoys punishing people. God is good, and God is on the side of the victim. God blesses the underdog, especially those who walk in an attitude of humility.

PERSONAL REFLECTIONS

1. Are you overly critical of others? Rank yourself on the scale below.

```
◄───────────────────────────────────────►
1                     5                   10
Not very critical     Somewhat critical   Very critical
at all
```

2. Has God ever dealt with you harshly as a result of your judgmental attitude? Explain.

_____

_____

_____

_____

_____

Take a moment to ask God to make you more humble and less critical of others. Confess any mistakes you have made in recent memory, then ask that you would be able to fully enjoy the forgiveness only God can give.

CHAPTER 9

WHEN WE ARE RIGHT TO JUDGE

WHEN JESUS SAYS, "First take the plank out of your own eye, and then you will see clearly to remove the speck from your brother's eye," He is not denying that there will be times in which we should help to remove the "specks" from the eyes of our brothers. Sometimes it is absolutely right to warn others about someone's behavior. For example, the apostle John, who has so much to say about loving one another, warned about a troublemaker in the church. (See 3 John 9–10.) Paul reported that Demas had forsaken him because he "loved this world" and said that Alexander the metalworker had caused him "a great deal of harm" (2 Tim. 4:10, 14). But referring to all who had deserted him, Paul advised, "May it not be held against them" (v. 16).

FACING OUR OWN FAULTS FIRST

It is an injustice when certain people are at large who have done and can still do great harm to others. This is why a person who is raped should testify in court; it is why a person who threatens the unity of the church should be dealt with. But there are basic principles that must be followed in this type of judgment and that allow justice to be carried out without violating the spirit of the seven principles of total forgiveness.

Jesus introduced this matter with a question: "Why do you look at the speck of sawdust in your brother's eye and pay no attention to the plank in your own eye?" (Matt. 7:3). This verse candidly shows how we tend to get upset over small issues (the "speck of dust") in another person's life and yet so easily overlook the big issues (the "plank") in our own lives. This lack of objectivity disqualifies us from being helpful. When we lose our objectivity, we render ourselves incapable of passing judgment on another person.

Fault-finding, then, is out of order. Jesus' rhetorical question forces us to confront our tendency to meddle over what gets our goat. The fault we see in someone else is what Jesus calls a "speck"—a little thing that annoys us. But the whole time we overlook our own very serious problems. Ironically, the cause of fault-finding, or meddling, is the plank in our own eye that we cannot see. *Plank* is Jesus' word for what is wrong with us; it is the sin in us, the evidence of our fallen nature. It is what makes us so eager to point the finger rather than to forgive.

The planks in our eyes cause poor eyesight; they magnify the specks of dust in others while simultaneously blinding us to our own faults. The planks in our eyes focus on and enlarge the weaknesses in others so that they appear much worse than they really are; in actuality, it is our weaknesses that are in operation, simultaneously magnifying (their faults) and blinding (us to our faults).

PERSONAL REFLECTIONS

1. Give an example of a "plank" you might have in your own eye. Then give an example of a "speck" in someone else's.

   _____

   _____

_____

_____

_____

2. Have you ever met a "professional speck-hunter"? Are
   you one? Why is it so tempting to point out specks
   while ignoring our planks? Explain.

_____

_____

_____

_____

HOW TO BEHAVE IF SOMEONE CRITICIZES US

What if someone meddles in your life? How do you respond?
Most of us find it hard to respond in a way that pleases God.
First, He calls us to maintain a sweet spirit. Never forget, "A
gentle answer turns away wrath, but a harsh word stirs up anger"
(Prov. 15:1).

Second, we are to agree with them. Usually there is a little bit
of truth in what a critic will say to us or about us. Even if you
can't find a way to agree, you can always say, "I see what you
mean."

Third, we should thank the person. This will not only defuse
his irritation, but it will also enable him to save face should he
be up to no good. In addition, we will avoid making an enemy
unnecessarily in the process.

What we must never do when being confronted is to defend
ourselves or try to impress the other person with how good or
right we are. We must never seek to punish or get even or make
him look bad. Ask him to pray for you! But do it in a noncomba-
tive manner, never sarcastically. Confess sincerely, "I need all the
help I can get." The principles of total forgiveness should enable
us to make friends, not lose them.

PERSONAL REFLECTIONS

1. Talk about a time someone confronted you or meddled in your life in an unwelcome way. What was your reaction? Was there truth in their criticism?

_____

_____

_____

_____

_____

2. Do you want to respond better the next time this happens? Explain what you plan to do.

_____

_____

_____

_____

_____

TIMES WHEN WE ARE PERMITTED TO JUDGE

Is Jesus telling us that we can be qualified to judge after all? Yes, sometimes we are. If we are able to remove the plank from our own eyes, we are apparently set free to remove the speck from another's eye.

We must be careful here. Some people with absolutely no objectivity about themselves will claim to be qualified judges on the premise that they have no planks in their eyes! I have actually met people who can look at you with a straight face and claim their right to judge because they got rid of their plank years ago! And if you question them, you will be accused of judging!

Are we to believe that Jesus is encouraging some of us to

judge on the basis that we no longer have a plank in our eyes? If so, we are back to square one; we can all go back to pointing our fingers! This is arguably the most delicate question of this book. We all face unjust situations every day. How long are we to tolerate wrongdoing? People will take unfair advantage of others. And there may be a feeling in your bones that someone should speak out against the injustices. But because we are told to forgive and not to judge, it may not seem to be the right thing to do. Jesus even went so far as to say, "But I tell you, Do not resist an evil person. If someone strikes you on the right cheek, turn to him the other also" (Matt. 5:39).

Who would be bold enough to say that he or she has no plank? I am certainly not that bold. Jeremiah 17:9 aptly describes my situation: "The heart is deceitful above all things and beyond cure. Who can understand it?"

When Paul says in Romans 7:18 that nothing good lives in him, I have to say, "That's me, too!" When he says in 1 Timothy 1:15, "Here is a trustworthy saying that deserves full acceptance: Christ Jesus came into the world to save sinners—of whom I am the worst," I am inclined to say, "That may have been true then, but now surely I am the worst."

If I must know that there is no plank in my eye before I can offer any sort of correction to or warning about an evil person, I have to say here and now that I am out of the picture! I will never be among those qualified to judge.

How can imperfect people judge other imperfect people? Is it possible? If not, doesn't the whole community break down as everyone does what they please with no recrimination?

It is possible to remove the plank in a limited way. Galatians 6:1 tells us, "Brothers, if someone is caught in a sin, you who are spiritual should restore him gently. But watch yourself, or you also may be tempted."

Let us say I have found out that a brother in my church has fallen into the sin of adultery. Am I qualified to approach him about his sin? In an absolute sense, no, because I am a sinner, too. As a matter of fact, without God's grace, I could very well see myself in his situation. But because I am not in an adulterous relationship, I have, in that particular area, removed the plank from my own eye. And the reason I am qualified to help is because I am not trying to find fault with him. I will let him know that I too am a sinner. I may not necessarily turn him around, but hopefully he will not resent my coming to him or see me as meddling. He will understand that I am concerned for his life and his spiritual state, not to mention the honor of God's name.

A few years ago two elders had the task of approaching a man in their church who was in an adulterous relationship. On their way to the man's home, one elder said to the other, "Do you believe that you too could fall into this sin?" The reply was, "No." The elder who asked the question then said, "You are not qualified to approach this man"—and the visit was canceled. The essential qualification for a spiritual confrontation is the attitude required by Paul in Galatians 6:1, one of humility and self-searching.

Here is a rule of thumb to follow: the one who is hardest on himself will probably be the gentlest with others. Those who are most aware of their own weaknesses are most likely to be able to help others. The one who doesn't moralize, but rather encourages others to become more like Christ, is the one most qualified to engage in the ministry of reconciliation and restoration.

A qualified person will avoid becoming emotionally involved in the situation; he has no personal ax to grind. His self-esteem is not connected to the situation. We are qualified to help another person only to the extent that we truly love and care for him. We cannot help if we are irritated with or annoyed by him.

For this reason, it is often persons who are not personally connected to a situation who are best able to help. Such persons will be sympathetically detached—that is, like those trained to offer professional help, they will have sympathy for the people involved without allowing any prejudice or emotional involvement. They cannot be fixated or obsessed with that person. Their only consideration will be the honor of God's name.

Jesus never tells us how to remove the plank from our own eye, possibly because such a removal is not possible in the absolute sense. But paying sufficient attention to our own planks will keep us from pointing the finger at others or meddling in situations where we do not belong.

Personal Reflections

1. When is it right to offer correction? Explain your thoughts.

_____

_____

_____

_____

2. Have you ever seen someone restored by gentle correction or confrontation? Have you seen someone destroyed by botched confrontation and accusation? Think about each incident. What would have made the second one produce better results?

_____

_____

_____

_____

3. Write a prayer asking God for wisdom in this area, as someday you may be called upon to correct or confront a brother or sister in Christ.

_____

_____

_____

_____

CHAPTER 10

THE ART OF FORGIVING AND FORGETTING

FIRST CORINTHIANS 13, the great love chapter of the Bible, is a perfect demonstration of the cause and effect of total forgiveness. The apex of this wonderful passage is the phrase found in verse 5: "[Love] keeps no record of wrongs."

Why do we keep records, even mental ones, when others wrong us? To use them later. "I'll remember that," we say—and we are true to our word. It usually comes up sooner rather than later. Although we may acknowledge with our minds the words of the Lord, "It is mine to avenge" (Rom. 12:19), we are really saying in our hearts, "God isn't doing His job." So we help God out by punishing that person who hurt us—whether it be a spouse, a relative, a church leader, an old schoolteacher, or an insensitive boss.

Love is a choice. It is an act of the will. Keeping a record of wrongs is also an act of the will—a choice not to love—and it is the more natural, easy choice for us to make. Our record of wrongs is often rehearsed through our words.

> Likewise the tongue is a small part of the body, but it makes great boasts. Consider what a great forest is set on fire by a small spark. The tongue also is a fire, a world of

evil among the parts of the body. It corrupts the whole person, sets the whole course of his life on fire, and is itself set on fire by hell.

—JAMES 3:5–6

The irony is that, instead of "getting something off our chests," our words can cause an uncontrollable fire to erupt and incinerate what remains inside us. And instead of that fire subsiding, it doubles, intensifies, and gets a thousand times worse in the end. It is a satanic victory, ultimately traceable to our keeping a record of wrongs.

This principle also applies to imaginary conversations—those internal dialogues with yourself in which you can't get "what they did" off your mind. You may fantasize what you will say or do to them, or what you might tell other people about them. This conversation may go on and on—and hours and days may pass when you neither accomplish anything nor feel any better!

One evening about eleven o'clock, as I was going to bed, I found myself having a conversation in my head about someone. I imagined I had the opportunity to spill the beans about this person. I pictured the scenario in great detail. I made myself look good and the other person look bad. But the Holy Spirit—miraculously—got into the matter. I heard Him say to me, "You can get a victory right now if you refuse to think about clearing your name." Even though the conversation existed only in my mind, I realized that I had an opportunity to triumph—in my spirit! It was a pivotal moment, because it was as if it were real—and I refused to say anything at all about the person. I had achieved victory. A peace entered my heart, and I knew then and there that I must never again enter into those imaginary conversations—unless I refused to vindicate myself.

For those who find such conversations therapeutic, I would only remind you to let your thoughts be positive and wholesome; keep no records of wrongs in your thoughts, and you will be less likely to expose such records by your words.

86

Personal Reflections

1. Have you ever had imaginary conversations that were eventually realized? What was the outcome? What did it tell you about the power of your thought life?

_____

_____

_____

_____

_____

_____

2. In your own words, why are internal dialogues with yourself so dangerous, even if you do not intend to speak them out? Read Romans 12:2 and jot down a few ideas about how it relates to this verse.

_____

_____

_____

_____

3. How tame is your tongue? Even if your physical tongue is tamed, is your thought life tamed, or does it run rampant? Rate your thought life on the scale below.

$\longleftarrow\!\longrightarrow$

1   10

Totally tame   Wild

4. What can you do to get your thought life and/or tongue under control? List at least three practical steps you will begin to take today.

_____

_____

_____

_____

_____

REFUSING TO KEEP A RECORD OF OUR RIGHTS

Not keeping a record of wrongs is also a refusal to keep a record of the things you have done right. It is just as dishonoring to God's grace to keep a record of your rights as it is to keep a record of others' wrongs. Why? Because it is a form of self-exaltation. You are implicitly saying, "I told you so," in order to make someone else look bad. It takes spiritual maturity to refrain from saying, "I told you so."

More than a few people not only keep a record of wrongs, but also have an even longer list of times when they have been right! We all want other people to know how right we have been. We want them to know that we said it first. It is amazing to me the advice that comes after the fact: "I knew it all along." "Do you see now how right I was?" "You should have listened to me." "I told you so!"

Love not only tears up the record of wrongs but also the list of rights. True forgivers destroy the record they might have used to vindicate themselves. If there is no record of rights lodged firmly in your head, you will not be able to refer to it later to prove how right you were. Forget what they did that was wrong, and forget what you did that was right. Paul said, "I do not even judge myself" (1 Cor. 4:3). I have often concluded that very few people really deserve the vindication they think they are entitled to. I can only say that, if vindication is truly deserved, then that vindication will surely come, for God is just.

Personal Reflections

1. Do you have a mental scorecard on which you are always the winner? Is everyone else a loser, according to your scorekeeping system? Explain.

_____

_____

_____

_____

_____

2. Is this a lesson you have heard before but have never seriously applied? What reasons have you used to allow yourself to keep a list of "rights"? What can you do now to banish those excuses and truly repent? Make a plan of action of how you intend to quit keeping that list.

_____

_____

_____

_____

_____

JIM BAKKER'S EXPERIENCE OF LETTING GO OF WRONGS

I once watched an extraordinary edition of *Larry King Live* on CNN. Before the eyes of millions, Jim Bakker and Tammy Faye Messner (formerly Tammy Faye Bakker) appeared together on television for the first time in fifteen years. Jim Bakker, the television evangelist, had been sentenced to forty-five years in prison for something, it turned out, he had not done. He was initially found guilty of deliberately misleading his television viewers, encouraging them to send in money to buy homes that did not exist. He sat in prison for many years before he was vindicated. And in the meantime, his wife, Tammy Faye, divorced him and married his best friend, Roe Messner.

Eventually Jim was totally vindicated of the charges and was released from prison. Five years later, Jim married his present wife, Lori. Larry King invited the four of them to be on his TV program. What an interesting show it turned out to be!

Each person had a story to tell—of deep, deep hurts and total forgiveness. Both Jim and Tammy, before Jim's imprisonment, had felt betrayed by the American minister who was almost entirely responsible for Jim being sentenced to prison. Both needed to forgive this minister. Tammy had to forgive Jim for his adulterous sexual encounter with a young woman—the episode that led to his downfall. Jim not only had to forgive the unjust witnesses and biased judge, who had sentenced him unfairly, but also his wife for marrying his best friend while he was in prison. This is to say nothing about the hurts that the other two participants—Roe and Lori—had experienced.

The amazing theme of the interview was how Tammy had completely forgiven Jim for his affair, and how Jim had completely forgiven Tammy for divorcing him. At one point Jim said, "The Bible is so clear. . . . When I began to study the words of Jesus Christ, I learned that He said if you don't forgive from the heart, forgiving everyone, you will not be forgiven. Christ said, 'Blessed are the merciful for they shall obtain mercy.' I needed mercy, I needed forgiveness, so I wanted to give out to others what I myself needed. . . . Whether she forgave me or not, you know, I had to forgive her. I had to forgive everyone."

Larry asked Jim to explain how they were all friends.

"Only God can help people truly forgive and go on," Jim said. "In the Book of Colossians it talks about that. Because of what Christ did, we are pure; we are without judgment on ourselves. When I first went to prison, I was even questioning, 'Where, God? Where are You?' But as I went through the months of studying the Word of God, I realized that prison was God's plan for me. God was saying, 'I want you to come aside and be with Me.' Everyone in the Bible, from Genesis to Revelation, has either been in a pit or a prison or the backside of the desert. They've all been through bad things. So bad things do happen to people—they happened to all the great men of God."

PERSONAL REFLECTIONS

1. Jim Bakker and Tammy Faye Messner experienced a public shame and devastation most of us won't have to go through. Have you ever gone through your own kind of extreme trials? What were they? When it was over, were you able to forgive those who had treated you egregiously?

_____

_____

_____

_____

_____

2. If you were wrongfully accused, abandoned, imprisoned, and rendered penniless, what would your response be? Would you "grow" out of it, as Jim Bakker has? Or would you collapse? Explain.

_____

_____

_____

_____

_____

FORGIVING OURSELVES

Jim Bakker never believed for a moment that he was guilty of financial dishonesty, but he knew he had erred in his sexual affair and his prosperity teaching. His biggest problem, he says, was forgiving himself.

Forgiving oneself means to experience the love that keeps no record of our own wrongs. This love is a choice, as we have seen, and to cross over to the place where we choose to forgive ourselves is no small step. So many Christians say, "I can forgive others, but how can I ever forget what I have done? I know God forgives me, but I can't forgive myself."

We must remember that forgiving ourselves is also a lifelong commitment. In precisely the same way that I must forgive others every single day, I must also forgive myself.

Forgiving yourself may bring about the breakthrough you have been looking for. It could set you free in ways you have never before experienced. I well remember one Sunday morning just before I was to preach at the eleven o'clock service. I had an argument with my wife, Louise. I should never have done it, but I stormed out, slamming the door in her face. Before I knew it, I was bowing my head on the upper platform at Westminster Chapel before several hundred people. I don't know what they were thinking, but I know what I was thinking: *I should not be here. I have no right to be here. Lord, how on earth could You use me today? I am not fit to be in this pulpit.* It was too late to send a note to Louise saying, "I'm sorry." There was no way to resolve the situation at that time. I could only ask God for mercy and try my best to forgive myself. I assumed I was about to deliver the biggest flop of a sermon in the history of Westminster Chapel. Never in my life had I felt so unworthy. But when I stood up to preach, I was not prepared for the help I got. God simply undergirded me and enabled me to preach as well as I ever had!

PERSONAL REFLECTIONS

1. Is there some action in the past for which you have been unable to forgive yourself? Why do you cling so tightly to the past? Have the vines of self-blame over-

taken your life and become a thorny fixture? Journal
your explanation.

_____

_____

_____

_____

_____

_____

2. What do you think it would it feel like if you totally let
yourself off the hook, as God already has?

_____

_____

_____

_____

_____

3. What is it like to live in total forgiveness *of yourself*?
Do you know anyone who lives this way?

_____

_____

_____

_____

_____

Ask God to point out any areas in which you still blame yourself. Then we will continue and conclude this topic in the next
chapter.

CHAPTER 11

Signs That You Haven't Forgiven Yourself

IF WE FEEL guilty, blame ourselves, and find that we cannot function normally—even though we have confessed our sins to God—it indicates that we haven't yet totally forgiven ourselves. The person who hasn't forgiven himself is an unhappy person— and is usually unable to forgive others.

Thus, my not forgiving myself will often backfire, and I will struggle to forgive others. Or my not forgiving others may result in a sense of shame that causes unforgiveness of myself. The irony is that the degree to which we forgive others will often be the degree to which we forgive ourselves; the degree to which we set ourselves free will often be the degree to which we forgive others.

What causes our inability to forgive ourselves?

Anger
We may be angry with ourselves. Joseph in the Old Testament said to his brothers, "And now, do not be distressed and do not be angry with yourselves for selling me here, because it was to save lives that God sent me ahead of you" (Gen. 45:5).

God doesn't want us to be angry with ourselves for our sins. Jesus forgives us in the same exact manner in which Joseph forgave his brothers; just as Joseph did not want his brothers to be angry with themselves, Jesus does not want us to be angry with ourselves.

I remember talking with a minister who told me about a sexual affair of another preacher. He went on and on about how disgusting and reprehensible this man's behavior had been. He wanted my opinion on what should be done. I said, "Don't tell anyone else; just pray for this man."

"Really?" asked this minister, who wanted me to enter into his feeling of disgust.

I repeated, "Say nothing."

"Really?" this man said again.

"Yes," I said. "It could happen to you if you were put in the same situation."

I remember feeling a little uncomfortable with that man. I said to myself, *If, God forbid, I ever fall into sin in any shape or fashion, this is the last man I would ever tell.*

A few years later the same minister came to me with a problem. He had become attracted to a woman in his congregation. I immediately recalled the previous conversation I had had with him—but I said nothing about it. I simply urged this man to break the relationship off—utterly and immediately. It ended, thankfully, and the man continued to preach. He confessed his sin to God and received forgiveness. But there is more: after this incident, his preaching became more tender and his general spirit was more gracious than self-righteous.

Some Christians who can't forgive themselves are, underneath it all, angry with themselves. But God can begin today to cause all that happened to fit into a pattern for good. Begin to forgive yourself. And don't feel guilty about doing so! God says, "Take your forgiveness and don't look back." God will take the wasted years and restore them to good before it is all over. It is just as Joel promised: "I will repay you for the years the locusts have eaten" (Joel 2:25).

Personal Reflections

1. Is there any choice you have made in your life that makes you instantly angry at yourself when you think about it? Talk about it, and tell what you do with this anger.

_____

_____

_____

_____

_____

_____

2. Are you generally an angry person? Rate yourself on the scale below.

1	5	10
Never angry	Usually angry	Always angry

3. What positive purpose does anger serve? Does God see anger that way? How can you mature in this area?

_____

_____

_____

_____

_____

_____

True guilt and pseudo-guilt

There are two kinds of guilt most of us will struggle with: true guilt (a result of our sin against God) and pseudo-guilt (when there is no sin in our lives). Sin that has been confessed to God is totally forgiven by Him, and any guilt we feel after that is pseudo-guilt.

> For his anger lasts only a moment,
> but his favor lasts a lifetime;
> weeping may remain for a night,
> but rejoicing comes in the morning.
>
> —PSALM 30:5

When we say, "I'm sorry," and mean it, that's enough for God. He doesn't beat us black and blue and require us to go on a thirty-day fast to supplement Christ's atonement. He convicts us of sin to get our attention, but having done that, He wants us to move forward.

There are also two kinds of this false guilt:

- When sin was never involved in the first place
- When sin has been forgiven

Pseudo-guilt—though it is false—is also very real; that is, we feel keenly guilty. But it is called pseudo-guilt because, when it is thought through, there is no good reason for feeling guilty.

Take, for example, a person who is driving a car when a child runs out into the street at the last second and is struck down. The guilt can be overwhelming, but there was no sin. It doesn't need to be confessed to God.

Another example of false guilt is missing out on an opportunity. I have a friend in Florida who had a chance to buy a property many years ago for $5,000. He turned down the offer. Today that property is worth over a million dollars. He feels guilty that he didn't use his money more wisely, but this is not true guilt.

The other kind of pseudo-guilt is when you have confessed your sins—you may have even repented deeply—but you don't feel forgiven. Once we have acknowledged our sin, we should accept our forgiveness and leave the rest in God's hands.

Over the years I have developed a sense of failure as a father.

Children spell the word *love* T-I-M-E. I wish I had given more time to TR and Melissa in those early years at Westminster Chapel. I now understand that putting them first—not my church or sermon preparation—would have resulted in the Chapel carrying on just as well, if not better. But it's too late now. For me to continue to feel guilty over this is not pleasing to God because He has already totally forgiven me. He wants me to accept my forgiveness and let Him restore the years the locusts have eaten. If I let myself dwell on my failure, I am giving in to pseudo-guilt—and sinning as I do it because I am dignifying unbelief. I must keep destroying the record of my wrongs—every day.

PERSONAL REFLECTIONS

1. What issue haunts you with pseudo-guilt?

_____

_____

_____

_____

_____

_____

2. Write a prayer that God will allow you to tell the difference between real guilt and pseudo-guilt and will help you escape the haunting shadow of the latter.

_____

_____

_____

_____

_____

Pride, self-righteousness, and self-pity

At the end of the day, our unforgiveness of ourselves may be traceable to pride. That is what is ultimately at work when we compete with the blood of Christ. We, in our arrogance and self-righteousness, cannot bear the Lord doing everything for us so graciously, so we think we must help Him out a bit. It is an abominable way to think. Our pride must be eclipsed by humility; we must let God be God and the blood of Christ do what it in fact did: remove our guilt and satisfy God's sense of justice.

Just as fear and pride are like identical twins, so are self-pity and self-righteousness. We feel sorry for ourselves and show it by not forgiving ourselves. That is why pseudo-guilt can develop into very real and heinous guilt before God. It is false guilt, since God says, "You're not guilty." We make it into real guilt when we in effect reply, "Yes I am."

The bottom line is this: not forgiving ourselves is wrong and dishonoring to God.

The sweet consequence of not keeping a record of all wrongs is that we let go of the past and its effect on the present. We cast our care on God and rely on Him to restore the wasted years and to cause everything to turn out for good. We find ourselves, almost miraculously, accepting ourselves as we are (just as God does) with all our failures (just as God does), knowing all the while our potential to make more mistakes. God never becomes disillusioned with us; He loves us and knows us inside out.

Can you do that? Having forgiven others, it is time to forgive yourself. That is exactly what God wants of you and me. It is long overdue: let the past be past...at last.

PERSONAL REFLECTIONS

1. List some of the things for which you need to forgive yourself.

_____

_____

_____

_____

_____

_____

Consider each one and consciously let go of your right
to feel guilty about it or hold a grudge against yourself.
Over the next few days let the feeling grow into something durable and lasting.

2. Write a prayer from your heart asking God to help you
in this endeavor.

_____

_____

_____

_____

_____

_____

CHAPTER 12

FORGIVING YOUR ENEMIES

NOT EVERYONE WE must forgive is an enemy. There are those we must forgive who either do not know they have hurt us or, if they do, would never have done so intentionally. Some of the people I have had to forgive the most were not my enemies at all. By this I mean that they were not trying to bring me down or hurt me. They were people I had hoped would help me. On one occasion I asked an old friend to write a commendation for a book I had written. He refused, partly because there wasn't enough in it he agreed with and partly because I was gaining a reputation for mixing with people of whom he didn't approve. This hurt. He was no enemy, but I had to forgive him. I have had to forgive those who felt a need to distance themselves from me because I don't echo their "party line." I have had to forgive those who no longer need me as they once did. All of these things hurt. The irony is that it is sometimes harder to forgive those who are not enemies, but who have hurt you deeply, than it is to forgive one who is indeed an enemy.

PERSONAL REFLECTIONS

1. Think of friends you have had to forgive. Was it harder to forgive them than to forgive an "enemy"? Explain.

_____

_____

_____

_____

_____

_____

2. Is it possible to have friendships without hurting or being hurt? Explain.

_____

_____

_____

_____

_____

_____

3. How specifically can you be a more forgiving friend?

_____

_____

_____

_____

_____

_____

WHEN YOU HAVE ENEMIES

If you have a real, relentless, genuine enemy—someone who is not a figment of your anxiety or imagination—you should see yourself as sitting on a mine of twenty-four-karat gold. Not everybody is that blessed! But if you have been blessed in that way, take it with both hands. You should take this person's picture, enlarge it, frame it, and thank God every time you look at it. Your enemy, should you handle him or her correctly, could turn out to be the best thing that ever happened to you.

What is an enemy? It is a person who either wants to harm you or who would say something about you so as to call your credibility or integrity into question. He would rejoice at your downfall or lack of success. He would not pray that God would bless you and prosper you, but instead he would sincerely hope that God would bring you down. An enemy hates you, although he might never say the word. He will use any other word or phrase: "loathe," "despise," " I just can't stand them," "They make me sick," "I can't stand the sight of them."

An enemy will "despitefully use you" (Matt. 5:44, KJV). Sometimes a Christian will be unscrupulous in business with another believer because he knows this particular Christian would never take him to court. (See 1 Corinthians 6:1–8.) He may say libelous things in print because he knows you will not sue.

An enemy will often persecute you. The Greek word for *persecute* simply means "to follow" or "to pursue." Enemies will pursue you because they are obsessed with you. King Saul became jealous of David because he had become more popular, and King Saul was more worried about the threat of David's anointing than he was of Israel's archenemy—the Philistines! Saul pursued David, but he never succeeded in killing him.

Enemies will speak badly about you to your boss, keeping you from getting that promotion or raise in pay; they will tell your friends about any indiscretions they might perceive in your life; they will go out of their way to keep you from succeeding and from being admired by the people in the office or at church.

What is more, if they are Christians they may deceive themselves into thinking that they are doing it for God and His glory! "They will put you out of the synagogue; in fact, a time is coming when anyone who kills you will think he is offering a service to God" (John 16:2). Persecutors don't kill with the sword or a gun; they do it with the tongue or pen. Perhaps sometimes you wish they would just physically kill you and get it over with!

When you know that a person is obsessed with you and is out to discredit you, you are very, very blessed indeed. This doesn't happen to everyone. You are chosen, for behind your enemy is the hand of God. God has raised up your enemy—possibly just for you! King Saul's pursuit of David was the best thing that could have happened to David at the time. It was a vital part of David's preparation to become king. God did David a very special favor: He raised up Saul to keep him on his toes, to teach him to be sensitive to the Spirit (1 Sam. 24:5), and to teach him total forgiveness. Saul was David's passport to a greater anointing.

PERSONAL REFLECTIONS

1. Do you have any known enemies? What have they done to prove they are your enemies?

_____

_____

_____

_____

_____

2. Characterize your response and relationship to these people thus far. How do you intend to change your response to them now? Make a plan for dealing with your enemies.

———————————————————
———————————————————
———————————————————
———————————————————
———————————————————
———————————————————

TOTALLY FORGIVING OUR ENEMIES

When you totally forgive your enemy, you have crossed over into the supernatural realm. Perhaps you are like me and wish you could excel in all the gifts of the Spirit; you wish you could have a hand in signs and wonders; you'd love to see your usefulness intensified and extended by a double anointing. The gifts are supernatural. But if you and I totally forgive one who is truly an enemy, believe me, we have just crossed over into the realm of the supernatural.

I believe we are talking about the highest level of spirituality that exists, a feat greater than climbing Mount Everest, for totally forgiving an enemy is to climb the spiritual Everest. It means the highest watermark in anyone's spiritual pilgrimage. Totally forgiving an enemy is as spectacular as any miracle. No one may even know, though. You quietly intercede for them in solitude. Only God, the angels, and the devil know.

And yet it is within reach of any of us. No high connections in government, business, or society are required. No particular cultural background is needed. No university education is needed. A high level of intelligence is not required. You and I can do something exceedingly rare: forgive an enemy (if we have one). And the blessing is beyond words to describe.

In the next chapter, we'll see specific steps for totally forgiving others. But before moving on, write a prayer asking God to bless anyone who has behaved like an enemy toward you—a rude clerk at the store, an aggressive driver, someone at church who opposes you for some reason, or even a family

member who is out to get you. In your prayer, thank God for
this blessing!

_____

_____

_____

_____

_____

_____

CHAPTER 13

How to Forgive—Totally

SINCE FORGIVENESS IS a choice, what is the next step? If we are persuaded that it is right and have decided to do it (and not look back), what next? The answer has already been given, but I restate the reasons here.

1. Make the deliberate and irrevocable choice not to tell anyone what they did.

As I said earlier, you may need to do this for therapeutic reasons, but only to one person who in turn will never reveal your heart. Otherwise, do not mention it; refuse to tell anybody.

This isn't necessarily easy sometimes, but when our motive is to hurt another person by telling on them, there is sin on our part. So do not tell it at all or in part; keep it quiet.

2. Be pleasant to them should you be around them.

Do not say or do anything that would make them anxious. Put them at ease.

3. If conversation ensues, say that which would set them free from guilt.

Guilt is most painful, and we can easily punish people by sending them on a "guilt trip." Never do that. Remember that Jesus doesn't want us to feel guilty. When we are going to be Jesus to another, then we will not want them to be angry with themselves. "Do to others as you would have them do to you" (Luke 6:31).

4. Let them feel good about themselves.

Not only does this mean never reminding them of their wrong and your hurt, but it also means helping them through any guilt they may have. You must behave as though you don't even think they did anything wrong! That is hard for all of us, but it must be done. Say whatever you can (as long as it is true) that will give that person a sense of dignity. That is the point of Galatians 6:1: "Brothers, if someone is caught in a sin, you who are spiritual should restore him gently. But watch yourself, or you also may be tempted." As long as there is a trace of self-righteousness and pointing the finger, your attempt at total forgiveness will backfire.

5. Protect them from their greatest fear.

If you are aware of some deep, dark secret and fear they have, they will probably know that you know. If they can tell by your graciousness that their secret will never be revealed—ever—to anyone, they will be relieved. You only tell them when you know they know what you know, and you are convinced this would make them feel better. If by reminding them it would obviously not make them feel better, don't even come close!

6. Keep it up today, tomorrow, this year, and next.

As we have said, total forgiveness is a lifelong commitment. Some days will be easier than others. There will come a time when you think you are completely over it and have won a total victory—only to find the very next day Satan reminds you of what they did and the utter injustice that they will be unpunished and never exposed. The temptation to bitterness will emerge. After all, we're not perfect! If we say we have no sin—that we are incapable of the same old bitterness—we are deceived (1 John 1:8).

This is exactly why I read Luke 6:37 every day: "Do not judge, and you will not be judged. Do not condemn, and you will not be condemned. Forgive, and you will be forgiven." All commitments to forgive need renewal. In my case, daily. I am not telling you that this is what you must do, but be warned: the devil is cunning. He will come through the back door unexpectedly and try to upset you for forgiving. When you forgave your enemy, you then and there removed that open invitation to the devil to get inside. Satan's favorite rationale is bitterness—he therefore will keep trying to get back into your thought life.

Whether it be Luke 6:37 or another way forward in your case—even if you aren't required to keep it up each day—I can tell you right now that it is only a matter of time before your commitment to forgive will need to be renewed.

7. Pray for them.

"But I tell you: Love your enemies and pray for those who persecute you" (Matt. 5:44). When you do this from the heart—praying for their being blessed and off the hook—you're there. It is not a perfunctory prayer, not a "We commit them to You" prayer, and certainly not a "O God, please deal with them" prayer. It is praying that God will forgive them—that is, overlook what they have done and bless and prosper them as though they'd never sinned at all.

I remember a church leader turning to me to pray about his son-in-law who had been unfaithful to the leader's daughter. He said to me that his own prayer was only this: that God would "deal" with this man. "This is where I have come to," he said to me, "that God will deal with him."

I understood what he meant, and I felt for him. I find what people do to our own offspring are the hardest things to forgive. I therefore understood what he was feeling. A few days later it was reported that this leader's son-in-law had been in a serious accident. This same church leader was on the phone, glad that the accident had happened. Now in this particular case there was nothing sinister in this euphoria. He simply hoped that the accident would wake up his son-in-law to put his marriage back together. It was so understandable.

But this is not what Jesus means. He is commanding us to pray that our enemy will be blessed. If, however, you should pray that they will be cursed or punished instead of being blessed, just remember that is how your enemy possibly feels about you. After all, have you ever been someone's enemy? Have you ever done something that brought a fellow Christian to tears and brokenness? If so, how would you like that person to pray for you? That God will deal with you? That God will cause you to have an accident? Yet how would it make you feel if they prayed that you would be blessed and let off the hook? That you would prosper as if you'd never sinned? Would you not like that? "Do to others as you would have them do to you" (Luke 6:31).

Jesus wants a sincere prayer from us. It is like signing your name to a document, having it witnessed, and never looking back. You are not allowed to tell the world, "Guess what I did? I have actually prayed for my unfaithful spouse to be blessed." No. It is quiet. Only the angels witness it, but it makes God very happy.

After all, every parent wants their children to get along with one another. No parent likes it when one child comes and squeals on the other and demands that they be punished. The poor parent is put on the spot. What gladdens the heart of every parent is when there is love and forgiveness. That is what we do for God when we ask that He bless and not curse. He told us to pray for our enemies, "that you may be sons of your Father in heaven. He causes his sun to rise on the evil and the good, and sends rain on the righteous and the unrighteousness" (Matt. 5:45).

PERSONAL REFLECTIONS

1. How far along are you in these seven steps? Which of these steps come easy? Which steps are still difficult?

_____

_____

_____

_____

_____

_____

2. Make a plan for tracking your progress along the road
   to forgiveness. How will you know that you are moving
   ahead? Explain.

_____

_____

_____

_____

_____

_____

THE FIVE STAGES IN PRAYING FOR OUR ENEMIES

There are five stages, or levels, of praying for one's enemy:

- DUTY. The first level is strictly based on obedience; you
  are doing it because you feel you have to.

- DEBT. You have reached the second level when you are
  so conscious of what you have been forgiven of that you
  cannot help but pray for your enemy. You don't want
  God to "spill the beans" on you, so you pray that your
  enemy too will be spared.

- DESIRE. You begin to pray for your enemy because it is
  what you really want.

- DELIGHT. This takes desire a step further. It is when you
  love doing it! You get joy from praying for and blessing
  your enemies.

- DURABILITY. This means that what you took on as a life-long commitment becomes a lifestyle. The thought of turning back or praying in a different way is out of the question. It has become a habit, and it no longer seems like something extraordinary. Jackie Pullinger said, "To the spiritual person the supernatural seems natural." What began as a duty and once seemed insurmountable is now almost second nature.

All this is done in secret, behind the scenes. You aren't allowed to get your reward or applause from people who may think, *Oh, isn't that lovely you would pray for your enemy like that!* No. It is a secret that must never be told. Enter into your place of prayer and shut the door behind you. "Then your Father, who sees what is done in secret, will reward you" (Matt. 6:4).

There are several consequences of praying for your enemies or persons who have disappointed you. The most obvious consequence is your reward in heaven. But another consequence is that—be warned—God may answer your prayer! "Oh, no!" you may say, "I only prayed for them because I was being obedient. Surely God would not actually bless and prosper that wicked person?" Well, He may indeed! The question is, will you still pray the prayer?

Another surprising consequence of your prayer is that—just maybe—your enemy may become your friend. That is what God did to us:

> God was reconciling the world to himself in Christ, not counting men's sins against them. And he has committed to us the message of reconciliation.
> —2 CORINTHIANS 5:19

You too may well win your enemy over by loving them and praying for him or her. "I don't want this person as a friend," you may say now. That's OK. We saw earlier that total forgiveness does not always mean reconciliation. Do not feel guilty if you don't want to become close friends. But in some cases this has happened. And if there is a reconciliation or a friendship that eventually results, that person may say to you, "You were brilliant the whole time. You were loving and caring, never vindictive." One rule of thumb to follow: treat your enemy now the way you will be glad you did should you become good friends.

The greatest positive consequence is the knowledge that you have pleased God. I want to be like Enoch, who was "commended as one who pleased God" (Heb. 11:5). Nothing pleases God more than our loving and praying for our enemies. It is significant that Job's troubles stopped when he prayed for his friends who were persecutors and tormentors during his suffering. "After Job had prayed for his friends, the LORD made him prosperous again and gave him twice as much as he had before" (Job 42:10).

Doing this is, of course, our duty—but it eventually becomes a delight.

PERSONAL REFLECTIONS

1. Where do your prayers for your enemies fall on this chart at present?

Duty	Debt	Desire	Delight	Durability

2. In practical terms, how do you intend to get better at praying for enemies until it becomes a lifelong delight?

_____

_____

_____

_____

3. Are there any unresolved issues of forgiveness you need to address? Explain.

_____

_____

_____

_____

_____

_____

4. What specific steps will you take to totally forgive?

_____

_____

_____

_____

5. Write a prayer summing up your specific requests for
help in this area. Ask God to honor your desire to
totally forgive.

_____

_____

_____

_____

NOTES

CHAPTER 1
CAN YOU LEARN TO FORGIVE?
1. Susan Pape, "Can You Learn to Forgive?" *London Daily Express* (June 5, 2000).

CHAPTER 2
WHEN IT HURTS TO FORGIVE
1. Gary Thomas, "The Forgiveness Factor," *Christianity Today* (January 10, 2000), 38.

Take the next step in your faith walk today.

We pray that God has encouraged and strengthened you with this autobiography. Dr. R. T. Kendall also has several other soul-refreshing messages that you won't want to miss!

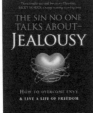
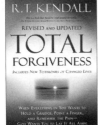

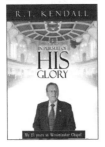

Overcome Envy and Live a Life of Freedom

Combining biblical depth with personal candor, R. T. Kendall shows you how to identify and get free from the crippling effects of jealousy
$14.99 / 978-1-59979-941-4

Forgive and Forget?

When everything in you wants to hold a grudge, point a finger, and remember the pain, God wants you to lay it all aside.

"This is a book that should be read around the world."
—D. James Kennedy, PhD., Senior Minister, Coral Ridge Presbyterian Church

$14.99 / 978-1-59979-176-0 (Paperback)

Fresh Anointing for You Today

R.T. Kendall helps you identify your current role in the kingdom. Learn how to wait for God's perfect timing, promotion, and fresh anointing in each season of your life.
$13.99 / 978-1-59185-172-1 (Paperback)

Life Lessons for Today

After 25 years at Westminster Chapel, R.T. Kendall has learned seven simple, yet amazing life lessons. In this message, he shares his wisdom and spiritual insights.
$19.99 / 978-1-59185-454-8

Visit your local bookstore today.